THE DECLARATION OF
INDEPENDENCE

THE DECLARATION OF
INDEPENDENCE

A Global History

DAVID ARMITAGE

HARVARD UNIVERSITY PRESS
Cambridge, Massachusetts
London, England
2007

Cataloging-in-Publication Data available from the Library of Congress

ISBN-13: 978-0-674-02282-9
ISBN-10: 0-674-02282-3

Contents

THE DECLARATION OF
INDEPENDENCE

Introduction

In the last public letter he wrote before his death in 1826, Thomas Jefferson offered an expansive vision of the Declaration of Independence, a document he had drafted half a century before. As he declined an invitation to attend the commemoration in Washington, D.C., of the fiftieth anniversary of American independence, Jefferson called the Declaration "an instrument, pregnant with our own and the fate of the world." He regretted that illness would keep him from a reunion with "the remnant of that host of worthies, who joined with us on that day, in the bold and doubtful election we were to make for our country, between submission or the sword." He would have "enjoyed with them the consolatory fact, that our fellow citizens, after half a century of experience and prosperity, continue to approve the choice we made. May it be to the world, what I believe it will be, (to some parts sooner, to others later, but finally to all,) the signal of arousing men to burst the chains, under which monkish ignorance and superstition had persuaded them to bind themselves, and to assume the blessings and security of self government."[1]

Jefferson died on July 4, 1826, two weeks after sending this letter. He had written it in the tones of a prophetic utterance surveying past and future from the very brink of death. He surely intended the letter to be made public, and so it soon was, in a Washington newspaper on his deathday. Yet this was not the very last of Jefferson's letters. A day after sending it on June 24, 1826, he wrote two more, one to his business agent in Richmond, Virginia, the other to a merchant in Baltimore, regarding a shipment of French wine that had just arrived from Marseilles and on which duty had to be paid.[2]

Jefferson's last public thoughts may have treated the afterlife of the American Revolution, but his last private instructions concerned the stocking of his wine cellar. Both looked to the future. Both also acknowledged that the young United States was tied to a wider world, whether as an exporter of revolutionary ideas or as an importer of luxury goods. As Jefferson well knew, any independent country had to be an interdependent country.

By the time of Jefferson's death, "half a century of experience and prosperity" had confirmed American independence as a political fact. Fifty years earlier, the Declaration had announced independence at a time when it had yet to be achieved and when it was still under vigorous assault by Britain. For almost four decades after 1776, Americans valued the successful fact of that independence more than they did the specific document that had declared it. It was only in the last decade of Jefferson's life that the Declaration began to be seen as the well-founded article of "American scripture" celebrated by Americans every Fourth of July then and since.[3]

The Declaration of Independence may have acquired special significance for Americans, but its power as a symbol was potentially global in extent, as Jefferson's prophecy in 1826 affirmed. Even during the former president's lifetime, the Declaration had already become something more practical than a symbol: it provided the model for similar documents around the world that asserted the independence of other new states. By the time Jefferson called the Declaration "an instrument pregnant with . . . the fate of the world" in 1826, it had already been joined by some twenty other declarations of independence from Northern and Southern Europe, the Caribbean, and Spanish America. Now, more than two centuries since 1776, over half the countries of the world have their own declarations of independence.

Many of these documents drew directly on the American Declaration for inspiration. They adopted and sometimes adapted specific phrases from the Declaration. More often, they took its structure as a model for their own. Many more such declarations were written without the flattery of direct imitation. All shared clear similarities, whether in their motivation, in their language, or in their form, that make it possible to consider them collectively and globally.

Before now, declarations of independence have not been treated as a global phenomenon.[4] The reasons for this are central to the definition of independence itself. At root, independence means political separation of the kind that the representatives of the United States asserted against King George III in 1776. More broadly, independence implies national distinctiveness and difference. Over time, separation and uniqueness nourish a sense of exceptionalism, especially for a country like the United States, born out of secession and endowed by its visionaries with a mission in the world. The authors of the Declaration had claimed independence only for themselves and not for others. Their specific and particular idea of independence would nonetheless assume near-universal significance in the centuries after 1776 as the American example spread across the world.

The American Declaration came to be seen as marking the beginning of a history separate from other national or imperial histories. Similarly, many other declarations of independence throughout the world became the property of particular communities that have celebrated their own declarations as charters of a special standing in the world. Almost by definition, the written embodiments of such exceptionalism are unlikely to be compared with other, similar documents. So it has proved with declarations of independence.

Multiple declarations of independence have been collected for comparison on only two occasions. The first was in 1955, in advance of a meeting of the Organization of American States in Washington, D.C., when reproductions and translations of the declarations of independence produced in the Americas and the Caribbean between 1776 and 1898 were compiled into a single volume.[5] The second sprang indirectly from the commemoration of the United States bicentennial in 1976, when scholars published a collection of independence documents from around the world that included declarations of independence as well as various other instruments of independence, such as bilateral agreements and legislative acts.[6] Both these moments quickly passed. The compilations they left behind apparently led to no further reflection on what might be learned from considering declarations of independence as a group and in the round.[7]

Many declarations of independence have given rise to their own rich hinterlands of analysis and discussion. Most such treatments have tended to address the documents' immediate origins rather than their place in longer, let alone broader, histories. In this respect, the American Declaration is at once typical and unusual. It is typical in that many scholars since the nineteenth century have scrutinized its creation in the summer of 1776 and its dissemination thereafter. Their work has revealed a dizzying variety of possible sources for the Declaration's language and inspirations for its form, as well as a wealth of information about how it was drafted, edited, and published. Much of their work has debated the various European sources for the Declaration's statements concerning natural rights or the right of revolution, whether in English political thought, Scottish moral theory, or Swiss philosophy, for example.[8] That debate has concentrated mostly on the Declaration's second paragraph and its "self-evident" truths; it has not been broadened to consider other elements in the Declaration, such as the meaning of the independence it claimed for the United States. Recovering that meaning will be a major concern of this book.

Americans have been exceptionally well informed about one of the key documents in their national history. They have also had the unique opportunity to learn just who in the United States read the Declaration, how they interpreted it, and with what political and legal consequences.[9] No other declaration of independence has had its domestic legacy traced so fully or so revealingly. What Americans and others interested in the fate of

the Declaration have so far lacked is any systematic attempt to trace its afterlife in the world beyond the United States.[10]

The Declaration of Independence is hardly alone among the major landmarks of American history in lacking such a global treatment of its legacy. America's growing sense of self-sufficiency and its apparent hegemony in world affairs for much of the twentieth century have bred lasting strains of forgetfulness and even ignorance about the American impact on the world and, until recently, about the world's impact on America. Many other nations have suffered similar forms of historical amnesia about their place in the world. The very prominence of the United States in international affairs, however, makes resistance to thinking of its history in global terms especially glaring. The world beyond America has always shaped the United States—as it also formed its pre-revolutionary colonial past—by immigration, the spread of ideas, or the exchange of goods, and by almost every other conceivable form of interaction over more than four hundred years.[11] The growing awareness of these interactions in the past has spurred Americans and non-Americans alike to "rethink American history in a global age."[12]

Putting American history into global perspective in this way can help to show that what we now call "globalization" is not a novel condition. As one historian has recently written, the move toward a global level of analysis "reveals the interconnec-

tedness and interdependence of political and social changes across the world well before the onset of the contemporary phase of 'globalization' after 1945."[13] It can also help us see that globalization has not been a single, frictionless movement toward planetary integration. Rather, it has moved in a series of discontinuous and distinct phases that have unfolded at different moments and in diverse places. Understanding globalization in this way makes it harder to produce triumphalist narratives of world history. It also makes it possible to compare discrete phases of globalization to see what they had in common as well as how they differed.[14]

This book, written in one moment of acute awareness about globalization, is about another such moment, more than two centuries ago. The generation of Europeans and Americans that came of age in the decades before 1776 was almost the first in human history to have ready access to a comprehensively global vision of their place in the world. That vision was the product of many linked developments: maritime exploration; the elaboration of interoceanic trade; the spread of European empires in the Atlantic, Indian, and Pacific Oceans; the diffusion of maps, histories, and travel accounts; and the ties created by the circulation and exchange of goods and ideas. It had also been greatly expanded by the titanic struggle between Britain and France for imperial dominance across the globe, known to Americans as the French and Indian War (1754–1763) and to Europeans as

the Seven Years' War (1756–1763), a conflict fought out over four continents and across three oceans.[15] The generation of 1776 thus grew up in a postwar world decisively shaped by imperial rivalry and global competition.

That generation's global vision was enshrined in the comprehensive histories of European commerce and settlement that burgeoned in the years around 1776: the Abbé Raynal's *Philosophical and Political History of the Settlements and Trade of the Europeans in the East and West Indies* (1770), Adam Smith's *Inquiry into the Nature and Causes of the Wealth of Nations* (1776), and the Scottish historian William Robertson's *History of America* (1777), to name only the most notable. Edmund Burke ecstatically wrote of Robertson's *History:* "The Great Map of Mankind is unrolld at once; and there is no state or Gradation of barbarism, and no mode of refinement which we have not at the same instant under our View."[16] Raynal strongly supported the revolt of the British colonies. Smith published his work in part as an intervention in the debate on the future of Britain's "great empire on the west side of the Atlantic. This empire, however, has existed in imagination only." In the closing pages of the *Wealth of Nations,* Smith demanded that "this golden dream" of empire be either realized or abandoned entirely.[17] For Robertson, American independence definitively marked the end of that dream. He brought his *History* to an abrupt end with the loss of the American colonies: as he lamented in 1784, "alas

America is now lost to the Empire and to me, and what would have been a good introduction to the settlement of British Colonies, will suit very ill the establishment of Independant States."[18]

The global connections portrayed in the great commercial and oceanic histories by Raynal, Smith, and Robertson had come home forcefully to the American colonists in the course of the imperial crisis of the 1770s. The fortunes of Virginia planters and Boston merchants were bound up with the fate of the English East India Company in South Asia by great skeins of credit and debt that ran through banks in London and Glasgow, as well as by the circuits of trade that brought China tea in East India Company ships to Boston harbor in December 1773 under terms set by the Westminster Parliament. The origins of the American Revolution cannot be fully understood without an appreciation of the worldwide webs within which the colonists were enmeshed in the years leading up to 1776.[19]

Traces of both anxiety and excitement about those connections—were they chains or links, shackles or bonds?—can be found even in the Declaration when it announced the states' intention to enter the international system on equal terms with the other "Powers of Earth." These thickening global connections, and the decisive shifts in the European state system and in the balance of power within the Atlantic world that they brought in their wake, challenged contemporaries to understand their world in innovative ways. In this context, it seems to be more than just a coincidence that the English legal philosopher Jeremy Bentham found it necessary in 1780—during the crisis of the American War—to coin "the word *international* . . . a new one, though, it is hoped, sufficiently analogous and intelligible," to describe "the mutual transactions between sovereigns as such" that he encompassed under the neologism "international law."[20]

Every generation gets the Declaration of Independence it deserves. Our own global moment merits a global history of the Declaration. Such a history can be pursued from the outside in, to bring universal perspectives to bear on particular moments, places, persons, or objects. It can also be written from the inside out, from the local and specific to the worldwide and the general. These approaches are not competing but complementary; indeed, each would be impossible without the other. One can find what a near-contemporary of the Declaration, the English poet William Blake, called "a world in a grain of sand." In the case of the Declaration, this means the traces of a wider world embedded in one relatively brief and pungent document. That document took on a life of its own as it circulated at home and abroad: out of its travels emerged another kind of global history, the history of its dissemination and reception. That history in turn spawned imitations and analogues of the Declaration.

A global history can also be written from the patterns

revealed by the emergence and accumulation of other declarations of independence. In this book, I pursue all three approaches to the global history of the Declaration of Independence as I examine successively the evidence of the world in the Declaration, the Declaration's fortunes in the late eighteenth- and early nineteenth-century world, and the myriad declarations of independence produced since 1776. The Declaration of Independence cannot help looking different when it is put into such multiple global perspectives.

No single document is so bound up with what it means to be an American and few words can sum up the American creed as succinctly as "the rights to Life, Liberty and the Pursuit of Happiness." Yet even in its earliest material forms, the Declaration offered evidence of connections with a wider world. It first appeared in print on July 5, 1776, as a single-sheet broadside for distribution and display. The printer of this version of the Declaration was a native Irishman, twenty-nine-year-old John Dunlap, who had migrated to Philadelphia from Tyrone, County Strabane, in 1757.[21] He printed most of the copies on Dutch paper that had been brought from England, the source of much of the colonies' paper in this period; his printing press and the type he used in it would probably also have been imported from Britain.[22]

The Declaration would not be signed until late July and early August 1776. Fifty-five delegates to Congress—nine of whom had been born in Britain or Ireland, and over a dozen educated outside the colonies, in England, Scotland, and France—put their signatures to the engrossed manuscript copy of the Declaration. They did so using an inkstand fashioned by another Irishman, Philip Syng, Jr., out of silver that would have been mined in Mexico or Peru.[23]

The earliest public versions of the Declaration thus arose from the intersections of politics and printing, the migration of individuals and the movement of goods, around an Atlantic world that over the course of the eighteenth century increasingly linked Europe, Africa, and the Americas into a single economic and cultural system. If such traces of the world beyond the North American colonies can be discovered in a document vested with so much significance as an icon of Americanness, then surely similar vestiges can be found throughout the various materials out of which American history is built.

I treat the Declaration of Independence variously as an event, a document, and the beginning of a genre. In the words of Carl Becker, one of its earliest students, the Declaration as an "event" was "the culmination of a series of revolutionary activities" expressed in the "document in which that event was proclaimed and justified to the world."[24] The Declaration's global history did not end—indeed, it had barely begun—in July 1776. The document inaugurated a genre of political writing that has persisted to the present day. By "genre" I mean a distinct but repeatable structure of argument and literary form. Similar documents, whether or not they are consciously or directly indebted to a specific original, become instances of such a genre. Literary genres can be as strict as a sonnet or as loose as a novel; utopias and constitutions, declarations of rights and declarations of independence, are among similar genres of political writing. They supply the forms that capture, and allow us to comprehend and criticize, similar ideas and events. They provide the recurring shapes assumed by documents arising from comparable circumstances.[25] Genres are born. They break apart and recombine with elements of other genres. Sometimes they die. Like the ideas they contain, they are both movable and mutable, and they do not recognize national borders.

The Declaration marked the birth of a new genre of political writing. Part of its genius—and a major reason for its later success as a model for other declarations—was its generic promiscuity. It combined elements of what would become three distinguishable genres: a declaration of independence, a declaration of rights, and a manifesto. The opening and closing paragraphs of the Declaration—beginning, respectively, "When in the Course of human Events . . ." and "We, therefore, the Representatives of the UNITED STATES OF AMERICA . . ."—made up the declaration of independence itself. The second paragraph, starting with the still more famous words "We hold these Truths to be self-evident," was closer to what would be recognized as a declaration of rights, especially in the wake of the French Declaration of the Rights of Man and the Citizen of 1789.[26] Finally, the list of grievances that made up the bulk of the Declaration had the features of a manifesto that publicly explained to the world the grounds for a revolutionary action.[27]

After its publication, the Declaration rapidly entered national and international circuits of exchange. Copies passed from hand to hand, desk to desk, country to country, often with (to us) remarkable speed, but sometimes with perhaps less surprising inefficiency and mishap. To some, the Declaration could easily be ignored, while others sought it out, pored over it, or painstakingly translated it out of its original language. To yet others, it was a subversive document in an age when treason and revolution could be ignited by papers as readily as by rebels. "The independence of the Anglo-Americans is the event most likely to accelerate the revolution that must bring happiness on earth," remarked the French royal censor the Abbé Genty in 1787: "In the bosom of this new republic are the true treasures that will enrich the world."[28] As if to fulfill this prophecy, for more than two centuries the Declaration provided others with just the template they would need to communicate their own political intentions to "a candid World."

Once the Declaration had embarked upon this international career, it broke loose from the circumstances of its birth. It took on a life of its own and became the model for what would in time become a global genre. No document before 1776 had ever been called a declaration of independence; in fact, the Declaration itself did not carry that title, nor did the word "independence" appear anywhere in its text. For months before July 1776, however, contemporaries had been speaking of the need for "an independency," a "declaration of independency," or a "declaration of independence." On July 8, 1776, Jefferson sent "a copy of the declaration of independence" to his fellow Virginian Richard Henry Lee.[29] There could be no doubt, then, that the document issued by the Continental Congress and dated July 4, 1776, was a "declaration" (as it called itself, in both its printed and manuscript versions), and that what it declared, first and foremost, was "independence." Once it had done so, and after it had traveled far and wide as a document, it could be imitated, plundered, and paralleled by the many other documents that constitute the genre of declarations of independence.

Urgent international pressures had compelled Congress to issue a declaration in the early summer of 1776. Accordingly, the Declaration reflected a range of concerns about security, defense, commerce, and immigration. As a document that announced the transformation of thirteen united colonies into the "United States of America," the Declaration marked the entry of those states into what would now be called international society. Its authors addressed it to "the Opinions of Mankind" in diplomatic and legal language designed to render it acceptable to its audience beyond America. The Declaration thereby reflected changing conceptions of the international community of the Atlantic world. It helped to change that community by expanding its boundaries westward into North America and by opening American commerce to a wider world outside the limits previously set to it by the laws of the British Empire.

The American Declaration, like its successor declarations, was a document of state-making, not of nation-formation. It declared that what had formerly been dependent colonies within the British Empire were now independent states outside that empire's authority. It did so without mentioning "Americans" or using the word "nation." Instead, it concentrated on the emergence of "one People" assuming a separate and equal station "among the Powers of the Earth" and declared that "these United Colonies are, and of Right ought to be, FREE AND INDEPENDENT STATES." The Declaration's statements regarding rights to "Life, Liberty and the Pursuit of Happiness" were strictly subordinate to these claims regarding the rights of states, and were taken to be so by contemporaries, when they deigned to notice the assertions of individual rights at all. Thus a contemporary report in August 1776 noted that when the Declaration was first read out to the Continental troops at Ticonderoga, in western Pennsylvania, "the language of every man's countenance was, Now we are a people! We have a name among the states of this world!" The first loyalty oath issued by the new United States similarly asked officials to "acknowledge the UNITED STATES of AMERICA to be Free, Independent and Sovereign States, and declare that the people thereof owe no allegiance or obedience to George the Third, King of Great-Britain."[30]

American and foreign audiences found many different meanings in the Declaration during the decades immediately following 1776. Shifting international contexts in those years—of war, revolution, and state-formation—helped to change even the American understanding of the Declaration's central message from an assertion of statehood to a declaration of individual rights. Meanwhile, the circulation of the Declaration outside the United States encouraged a wider debate about the rights of states—especially new states, like the United States—to enter the international arena. The claims regarding individual rights in the Declaration's second paragraph played little part in these broader discussions. They would not be seen as crucial to the Declaration's meaning for an international audience until the advent of a global rights movement in the second half of the twentieth century.

The Declaration's enumeration of the rights of the former colonies "to do all [the] Acts and Things which INDEPENDENT STATES may of right do" drew attention to features of the state within the international realm. The conception of the state found in the Declaration was Janus-faced, as it is in most standard definitions of the state, classically encapsulated in the 1933 Montevideo Convention on the Rights and Duties of States as the possession of a permanent population, a defined territory, and a government, and the capacity to enter into relations with other states.[31]

The Declaration affirmed the existence of a population ("one People") and implied a form of government, but it did not define a territory. Instead, it stressed firmly the capacities of the United States as international actors alongside other such actors. My analysis in this book will follow this emphasis in the Declaration by highlighting the outward-looking rather than the inward-looking face of the state. Thus I downplay nations—as well as nationalism and national identity—in pursuit of a history concerning the relations of states with other states: how they have been created, by what criteria they have been recognized, and what the consequences of their proliferation have been.

States were not always the primary units of global politics that they had become by the latter half of the twentieth century. They faced competition from both larger and less well integrated political organizations in the form of empires.[32] In the last quarter-century, states have been rapidly outnumbered by proliferating nongovernmental organizations and multinational corporations.[33] They have also often had to confront challenges from substate groups or peoples claiming to be nations, in the sense of cultural communities based on the mutual recognition of commonality among their members. Yet we should not fall into the nationalist assumption of identifying states with nations as "nation-states." As Ernest Gellner has noted, "nations, like states, are a contingency, and not a universal necessity. . . . Moreover, nations and states are not the *same* contingency. . . . The state has certainly emerged without the nation. Some nations have certainly emerged without the blessings of their own state."[34]

The story of how the world came to be so thickly populated with states has hardly begun to be told.[35] Assembling and analyzing declarations of independence is an economical way to sketch the outlines of that much grander narrative. In order to assert their own statehood, most of the world's present-day states had at some point in the last two centuries declared their independence of the larger units that had once contained them. They sought confirmation of their standing alongside other such states by justifying their secession and, in some cases, their recombination with other territories and peoples. In short, they declared their possession of sovereignty, both internally, over all their own people, and externally, against all other states and peoples. More than one hundred declarations of independence have been issued since 1776, indicating a great political transformation of the last two centuries: the gradual emergence of a world—our world—of states from an earlier world dominated by empires. Considered in a series and as a genre, those declarations point up the stages of that epochal transition better than any other set of historical documents can.

The primary purpose of the American Declaration, like that of most declarations of independence that have been issued since 1776, was to express the international legal sovereignty of the United States. Thus Jefferson recalled in May 1825 that

> an appeal to the tribunal of the world was deemed proper for our justification. This was the object of the Declaration of Independence. Not to find out new principles, or new arguments never before thought of, not merely to say things which had never been said before; but to place before mankind the common sense of the subject, in terms so plain and firm as to command their assent, and to justify ourselves in the independent stand we are compelled to take. Neither aiming at originality of principle or sentiment, nor yet copied from any particular and previous writing, it was intended to be an expression of the American mind.[36]

Jefferson was perhaps too modest in his assessment. The Declaration was innovative in two ways that would have far-reaching consequences. First, it introduced "the United States of America" to the world; second, it inaugurated the very genre of a declaration of independence. No previous public document had used the name "the United States of America": in the months immediately before July 4, 1776, and even within the text of the Declaration itself, the political bodies represented at the Continental Congress had been generally called the "United Colonies."[37] Yet the earliest printed text of the document was explicitly called "A Declaration By the Representatives of the United States of America, in General Congress Assembled."

John Dunlap's broadside highlighted only three terms in its main text by means of capital letters: "the UNITED STATES OF AMERICA" in "GENERAL CONGRESS" assembled as they declared themselves to be "FREE AND INDE-PENDENT STATES." The formal manuscript copy of the Declaration produced later in July 1776 to be signed by all the delegates highlighted these same words. They appear in a distinctive italic script that draws attention to their significance. So faded is this manuscript of the Declaration now on display at the National Archives in Washington, D.C., that these are almost the only clearly legible parts of the text. That is only appropriate, for these words made up the central message of the Declaration as an assertion of sovereignty as independence.

This is what the Declaration of Independence declared: that the former United Colonies were now "the United States of America" because they were "free and independent states." No document in world history before 1776 had made such an announcement of statehood in the language of independence. A great many later documents would do just that. Indeed, the global history of the two centuries after 1776 would show that creating the flexible instrument with which others could declare their independence proved to be as momentous an innovation in its own way as ushering "the United States of America" onto the world stage in July 1776 had been.

CHAPTER ONE

The World in the
Declaration of Independence

So apparently familiar are the words of the Declaration of Independence that it is easy to forget what it was the Declaration declared. Ask most Americans—and no doubt many non-Americans—to quote the opening lines of the document and they will likely reply, "We hold these truths to be self-evident, that all Men are created equal, that they are endowed by their Creator with certain unalienable Rights, that among these are Life, Liberty and the Pursuit of Happiness." Just how those rights might have been connected to independence, few would now stop to ask.

"Self-evident truths"; "all men are created equal"; "unalienable rights"; "Life, Liberty and the Pursuit of Happiness": these are ringing words and noble sentiments, to be sure, but they are not in fact what the Declaration proclaimed in 1776. Even Abraham Lincoln, speaking in 1857, admitted: "The assertion that 'all men are created equal' was of no practical use in effecting our separation from Great Britain; and it was placed in the Declaration, not for that, but for future use."[1]

The Declaration would have been a document without a future had it failed in its central purpose of declaring independence. Had the Declaration been entirely ignored (as by many it was); had its fundamental claims been decisively refuted (as some thought they had managed to do); and had American independence been nipped in the bud by British military force (as it could very well have been), then few might now recall those supposedly "self-evident" truths.

To see what the Declaration did declare, it will be helpful to recall the structure of the document. For the Declaration was an announcement in the form of an argument, possibly patterned according to rules of logic that Thomas Jefferson—its primary drafter—had learned during his student days at the College of William and Mary in Virginia.[2]

The Declaration fell into five parts. Its initial premise, as stated in the opening paragraph, was that "a decent Respect to the Opinions of Mankind" required that "one People" breaking away from another should declare their reasons for doing so. Its secondary premises, stated in the now more famous second paragraph, held to be self-evident the truths

> that all Men are created equal, that they are endowed by
> the Creator with certain unalienable Rights, that among
> these are Life, Liberty and the Pursuit of Happiness.—
> That to secure these Rights, Governments are instituted
> among Men, deriving their just Powers from the Consent
> of the Governed, that whenever any Form of Government
> becomes destructive of these Ends, it is the Right of the
> People to alter or to abolish it, and to institute new Gov-
> ernment, laying its Foundation on such Principles and or-
> ganizing its Powers in such Form, as to them shall seem
> most likely to effect their Safety and Happiness.

Violations of basic rights like life, liberty, and the pursuit of
happiness could justify a separation only if they could be shown
to amount to "a long Train of Abuses and Usurpations." Only
then would a people be justified in seeking "to provide new
Guards for their future Security."

The third and longest part of the Declaration listed the
alleged "repeated Injuries and Usurpations" committed by
George III as "Facts . . . submitted to a candid World" in evidence of just such a train of abuses. The penultimate section
stated that those grievances had gone unredressed by "our British Brethren," so that "we must, therefore, acquiesce in the Necessity, which denounces our Separation, and hold them, as we
hold the rest of Mankind, Enemies in War, in Peace, Friends."

Separation from Great Britain could be justified both logi-

cally and historically. Accordingly, the Declaration concluded in
its fifth and final part that "these United Colonies are, and of
Right ought to be, FREE AND INDEPENDENT STATES." It
was to affirm this conclusion that the representatives assembled
in Congress resolved to "pledge to each other our Lives, our
Fortunes, and our sacred Honor."

The Declaration's opening and closing paragraphs clearly affirmed the entrance of a new actor ("one People") or actors
(thirteen "FREE AND INDEPENDENT STATES") onto the
world stage. The document's very first sentence stated truths
about that world so self-evident that they apparently needed no
justification or elaboration:

> When in the Course of human Events, it becomes neces-
> sary for one People to dissolve the Political Bands which
> have connected them with another, and to assume among
> the Powers of the Earth, the separate and equal Station to
> which the Laws of Nature and of Nature's God entitle
> them, a decent Respect to the Opinions of Mankind re-
> quires that they should declare the causes which impel
> them to the Separation.

Packed into this sentence was a set of assumptions about eighteenth-century international politics.[3] The most fundamental
was the existence of a group of political bodies ("the Powers of
the Earth") that interacted with one another according to cer-

tain external rules ("the Laws of Nature and of Nature's God"). They were entitled to do so for two main reasons: because they were separate from—or independent of—one another, and because they were equal in station to one another. Their number was not closed or fixed; from time to time, it could expand to include any "People" that had been compelled to become separate and thereby wished to claim equal standing with the existing powers. Like any public made up of discrete political persons, however, this community of earthly powers possessed opinions that needed to be informed and respected. Thus its members communicated with one another formally by means of public documents such as the Declaration itself.

The Declaration's concluding paragraph enumerated the rights possessed by those states that had successfully achieved their independence and equality:

> [T]hese United Colonies are, and of Right ought to be, FREE AND INDEPENDENT STATES . . . and that as FREE AND INDEPENDENT STATES, they have full Power to levy War, conclude Peace, contract Alliances, establish Commerce, and to do all other Acts and Things which INDEPENDENT STATES may of right do.

This list of the corporate rights of states was as open-ended as the roster of individual rights found earlier in the Declaration, which had stated that "all Men . . . are endowed by their Cre-

ator with *certain* unalienable Rights . . . *among these* are Life,
Liberty and the Pursuit of Happiness" (my emphases). The
Declaration specified the powers of states—war and peace,
treaty-making, and commerce—without foreclosing the need
to exercise other, similar powers should the need arise. With
that precise but flexible declaration of rights, the representatives of the United States announced that they had left the
transnational community of the British Empire to join instead
an international community of independent sovereign states.

The Declaration of Independence was therefore a declaration of interdependence. By issuing it, members of Congress
showed their "Respect to the Opinions of Mankind." They submitted the facts of their case to "a candid World," meaning
an unprejudiced world. And they pledged to treat the British
"as we hold the rest of Mankind, Enemies in War, in Peace,
Friends." The Declaration may have spoken on behalf of Americans through the voice of their congressional representatives,
but they were not the audience to which the text implicitly directed its argument. That was instead the "Opinions of Mankind," the collective public opinion of the powers of the earth.

The very term "declaration" would have implied as much. To
be sure, the word did have technical meanings within seven-
teenth-century English history and eighteenth-century English
law. Historically, a declaration was a public document issued
by a representative body such as Parliament; by calling its doc-

ument a "Declaration," the Continental Congress implied that it possessed the same sort of power to issue such documents as did the British Parliament.[4] Legally, what the leading eighteenth-century English lawyer Sir William Blackstone had called in 1765 "the *declaration, narratio,* or *count*" was the form "in which the plaintiff [in a civil trial] sets forth his cause of complaint at length." Only the third section of the American Declaration—the charge-sheet of grievances against the king—amounted to a declaration in this sense.[5]

In contemporary diplomatic parlance, a declaration meant a formal international announcement by an official body, "either by a general manifesto, published to all the world; or by a note to each particular court, delivered by an ambassador."[6] This is of course now the main meaning of "declaration" in terms like "declaration of war" or, indeed, "declaration of independence."[7] The Declaration of Independence possessed elements of all three forms of declaration. In its language, its form, and its intent, it most closely approximated "a general manifesto, published to all the world."

The Declaration was the culmination of a series of documents designed by the Continental Congress to shape the "Opinions of Mankind" across the British Empire (before July 1776) and then in the wider world (by the Declaration itself). Before issuing the document, Congress had produced some fifteen other state papers in the form of letters, petitions, pro-posals, addresses, and a speech, but it had issued only one other "declaration" as a formal precedent for the Declaration of Independence: the "Declaration by the Representatives of the United Colonies . . . Seting Forth the Causes and Necessity of Their Taking Up Arms" of July 6, 1775. Thomas Jefferson was one of the primary drafters, along with Pennsylvania delegate John Dickinson, of this earlier declaration. In it, they had acknowledged "obligations of respect to the rest of the world, to make known the justice of our cause" and had "exhibit[ed] to mankind" the plight of a wronged people.[8]

Like the Declaration of Independence, the "Declaration . . . [on] Taking Up Arms" marked a decisive turning point in the struggle between Britain and its American colonies: in this case, the move by the colonists to formal armed conflict. It, too, had been addressed to the judgment of a wider world, with the reassurance that "we have not raised armies with ambitious designs of separating from Great-Britain, and establishing independant states"; accordingly, Congress rapidly dispatched the document across the Atlantic to be printed in London newspapers. Congress's other state papers had been addressed variously to the British people, the inhabitants of Quebec, the people of Ireland, the Assembly of Jamaica, the Six Nations of the Iroquois Confederation, the province of Canada, and to Lord North and the king. Only one, in October 1774, had been addressed to the inhabitants of the colonies themselves. Even that document had been composed with the expressed hope of making "the strongest recommendation of their cause to the rest of mankind."[9]

The Declaration's change of implied audience in July 1776—from particular communities within the British Empire to "the candid world" at large—enacted the central claim of the work itself: that the United Colonies had ceased to be members of the British Empire and now stood alongside "the Powers of the Earth." In fact, for almost two years before making the Declaration, Congress had been exercising most of the rights claimed for the United States in that document. It had been negotiating with British representatives, appointing agents to pursue its interests in Europe, corresponding with foreign powers, and seeking various kinds of aid for the revolutionary cause.[10] For supporters of a declaration in Congress, therefore, "the question was not whether, by a declaration of independence, we should make ourselves what we are not; but whether we should declare a fact which already exists."[11]

For some, the Declaration itself was only the last in a series of acts that had severed the connection between Britain and the United Colonies in the months before July 1776. In August 1775, George III had already declared by proclamation that the American colonists were rebels, and hence outside his monarchical protection. Parliament had confirmed this royal proclamation in its Prohibitory Act of December 1775. John Adams, writing in March 1776, cautioned a correspondent against confusing mere freedom of trade with full-blown international independence: "Independency is an Hobgoblin, of so frightfull Mein, that it would throw a delicate Person into Fits to look it in the Face." Only the political dissolution of the bonds of empire could amount to such a fearsome step. Moreover, Adams thought that dissolution had already been effected by "the prohibitory Act, or piratical Act, or plundering Act, or Act of Independency." "It is a compleat dismemberment of the British Empire," Adams wrote. "It throws thirteen Colonies out of the Royal Protection, levels all Distinctions and makes us independent in Spight of all our supplications and Entreaties . . . But it is very odd that Americans should hesitate at accepting such a gift."[12] They would not hesitate for long. Although they were now rebels in the eyes of the British king and Parliament, they were not yet legitimate belligerents in the view of the rest of the world.

In order to turn a civil war within the British Empire into a war between states outside the empire, it was necessary to create legitimate bodies of combatants—that is, states—out of individual rebels and traitors. This was the motive behind the resolution that Richard Henry Lee moved in Congress on behalf of the Virginia delegation on June 7, 1776: "That these United Colonies are, and of right ought to be, free and independent States, that they are absolved from all allegiance to the British

Crown, and that all political allegiance between them and the State of Great Britain is, and ought to be, totally dissolved."

The international context of this resolution, effectively Congress's original declaration of independence, was evident from the rest of Lee's motion: "That it is expedient forthwith to take the most effectual measures for forming foreign Alliances. That a plan of confederation be prepared and transmitted to the respective Colonies for their consideration and approbation."[13]

This resolution led to the creation of three interlocking committees that shared both personnel and purposes. One was charged with writing a declaration of independence, another with drafting a model treaty of commerce and alliance, and a third with drawing up articles of confederation. Each of these documents was designed to be an expression of state sovereignty under the contemporary law of nations. The Declaration of Independence defined it. The Model Treaty would enact it.[14] The Articles of Confederation safeguarded it for each of the thirteen states in Article II ("Each State retains its sovereignty, freedom and independence"), but confined its international expression to Congress alone (in Articles VI and IX, which gave Congress "the sole and exclusive right and power of determining on peace and war").[15]

The need for recognition and assistance from other European powers had become ever more pressing since the autumn of 1775. In October 1775, John Adams wondered if foreign

courts might not rebuff American envoys: "Would not our Pro-
posals and Agents be treated with Contempt?"[16] Richard Henry
Lee similarly noted in April 1776 that "no state in Europe will
either Treat or Trade with us for so long as we consider ourselves subjects of G[reat] B[ritain]. Honor, dignity, and the customs of states forbid them until we rank as an independant
people."[17] Therefore it was necessary for the colonists to create
juridical bodies with which the European powers could legitimately conduct commerce and enter into alliances.

The most extensive presentation of the case for independence according to "the customs of states" came in January
1776 in the closing pages of Thomas Paine's best-selling pamphlet *Common Sense*. Paine argued that "nothing can settle our
affairs so expeditiously as an open and determined declaration
for Independence." Only independence would permit a media-
tor to negotiate peace between the United States and Great
Britain; without such mediation, "we may quarrel on for ever."
Foreign alliances could not be secured without it: France and
Spain would hardly support the colonies if they were to be
asked only to aid reconciliation with Britain. Charges of rebellion would also persist if independence were not declared: "we
must in the eye of foreign Nations be considered as Rebels."
Moreover, it was essential for a "manifesto to be published, and
despatched to foreign Courts," explaining colonial grievances,
the lack of redress, and the necessity of separation, "at the same

time assuring all such Courts, of our peaceable disposition towards them, and of our desire of entering into trade with
them." Until such a manifesto was dispatched, "the custom of
all Courts is against us, and will be so, until by an Independance, we take rank with other Nations."[18]

Throughout the spring and early summer of 1776, Paine's
arguments echoed in the various instructions, addresses, and
resolutions that local bodies throughout the colonies sent to the
delegates at the Continental Congress. For example, in April
1776, North Carolina's delegation was urged "to concur with
the Delegates of the other Colonies in declaring Independency,
and forming foreign alliances," and delegates from Charlotte
County, Virginia, were directed "to cast off the *British* yoke, and
to enter into a commercial alliance with any nation or nations
friendly to our cause." In the following month similar instructions came from Malden, Massachusetts, to express "the ardent
wish of our souls that *America* may become a free and independent State," and in June 1776 delegates from Connecticut were
instructed "to declare the United Colonies free and independent States."[19]

These instructions, like the Declaration itself, faithfully combined two arguments Paine had made so forcefully in *Common
Sense:* that the American colonies should be independent and
that they should be nonmonarchical republics, that is, "free . . .
States." By the end of the sixteenth century the word "state" had

taken on its recognizably modern meaning of an impersonal political power distinct from its holder. In anglophone political language, the term "free state" had come to mean specifically a nonmonarchical regime like the "Commonwealth and Free State" created after the execution of the English king Charles I in 1649.[20] As the American historian David Ramsay noted on the second anniversary of independence in 1778, "Independence has been the fruitful parent of governments formed on equal principles . . . While we were dependent on Britain, our freedom was out of the question; for what is a free state, but one that is governed by its own will?"[21] "Free and independent states" were thus republican governments, outside any allegiance to the British Crown and operating under the prevailing norms of the law of nations.

The standard guide to those norms available in 1776 was the compendious work by the Swiss jurist Emer de Vattel, *The Law of Nations* (1758).[22] Vattel's legal handbook had been a product of the early stages of the Seven Years' War. He wrote it in French, the prevailing language of European diplomacy, but it was almost immediately translated into English on its publication. Thereafter, it became the standard text on the subject in Europe and the Americas for more than half a century, with the result that its definitions of key terms in what we would now call international law and international relations became standard within the world of European—and, increasingly, also American—diplomacy.[23]

Vattel made independence fundamental to his definition of statehood:

> Every nation which governs itself, under any form whatsoever, without dependency on any foreign country, is a *sovereign state*. Its rights are by nature the same as those of every other state. These are the moral persons who live together in a natural society subject to the law of nations. For any nation to make its entrance into this great society, it is enough that it should be truly sovereign and independent, that is to say, that it governs itself under its own authority and its own laws.

Such independent sovereign states took on the qualities of the persons who comprised them: "Nations being composed of people naturally free and independent *(libres & indépendans)* and who, before the establishment of civil societies lived together in a state of nature, nations, or sovereign states, must be considered as if they were free persons who co-exist in the state of nature." From this fact, Vattel derived two overarching laws imposed upon all states: that they should contribute to the happiness and perfection of all other states; and that, because as states they are mutually free and independent *(libres & indé-pendantes les unes des autres),* they must leave one another in the peaceful enjoyment of their liberty. Vattel argued that, because states are free, independent, and equal *(libres, indépendantes, egales),* they must enjoy a perfect equality of rights. Such rights could not trump the laws of nations: all states might be free and independent *(libres & indépendantes),* but they were still bound to observe the laws of society that nature had established among them.[24]

No writer on the law of nations before Vattel had so consistently—and persistently—emphasized freedom, independence, and interdependence as the condition of states in their relations with one another. The authors of the American Declaration would soon adopt his repeated insistence that states were "free and independent" as the conception of their own states' condition. By doing so, they enacted Vattel's central contention that—in the words of his contemporary English translator— "independence is ever necessary to each state"; to secure that independence "it is sufficient that nations conform to what is required of them by the natural and general society, established among all mankind."[25] In due course, this would become the standard modern definition in international law of independence as "the capacity to enter into relations with other states."[26]

It was no coincidence that the conception of statehood as independence found in the Declaration of Independence resembled Vattel's so closely. In October 1774, James Madison had been informed that "Vattel, Barlemaqui Locke & Montesquie[u] seem to be the standar[d]s to which [Congress] refer either when settling the rights of the Colonies or when a dispute arises on the Justice or propriety of a measure."[27] Just over a year later, in 1775, Benjamin Franklin sought out the latest edition of Vattel's work for the benefit of Congress because "the circumstances of a rising state make it necessary frequently to consult the law of nations." Franklin obtained three copies of the book, which he dispatched to the Library Company of Philadelphia, to the Harvard College library, and to the Continental Congress itself. (Congress's copy has been lost, but the other two copies remain in the libraries to which Franklin sent them.) The work was immediately useful: as Franklin informed Vattel's editor, C. G. F. Dumas, in December 1775, it "has been continually in the hands of the members of our congress, now sitting."[28] The Declaration's vision of "Free and Independent States" assuming the "station to which the laws of nature and of nature's God entitle them" owes an obvious debt to Vattel's conception of states as free and independent under the laws of nature. Thus Franklin's words were not idle flattery.

The relative novelty in 1776 of the definition of international statehood as freedom and independence is obvious if one compares the American Declaration with two earlier documents retrospectively baptized as declarations of independence: the Declaration of Arbroath (1320) ("the Scottish Declaration of Independence") and the Dutch Act of Abjuration (1581) ("the Dutch Declaration of Independence"). The Declaration of Arbroath was addressed in the name of Scottish earls and barons to Pope John XXII, urging him to use his influence to convince the English king, Edward II, to enter peace negotiations with Robert Bruce, the king of Scots. The document asserted Scottish freedom on the basis of the historic continuity of the Scots nation and a conception of liberty drawn from the Roman historian Sallust. Its claims were thus backward-looking and defensive.[29] The document was never called a declaration of Scottish independence before the twentieth century: that recent pedigree did not deter the United States Congress from resolving in 1998 that the Declaration of 1776 had been modeled on that "inspirational document" of 1320, or from reaffirming that connection almost every year since in resolutions from both House and Senate in favor of marking a National Tartan Day on April 6, the date when the Arbroath declaration was signed.[30]

The Dutch Act of Abjuration *(Plakkaat van Verlatinge),* by which the States General cast off their allegiance to King Philip of Spain in July 1581, had abjured the sovereignty of King Philip but sought in his place "another powerful and merciful prince to protect and defend these provinces": it was, in this sense, a declaration of prospective dependence upon a new sovereign, the duke of Anjou.[31] The document was also based on historic and contractual rights that had been guaranteed and regularly reinforced since the fourteenth century, rather than on an appeal to natural law or other abstract rights outside of history and beyond positive agreement. However, the form of the American Declaration—with its assertion of a right to throw off the sovereignty of a tyrannous prince and its enumeration of grievances—was still close enough to that of the Dutch Act for the pro-British (and anti-American) Dutch stadtholder William V, prince of Orange, to call the Declaration in August 1776 but "the parody of the proclamation issued by our forefathers against King Philip II."[32]

There is at best only circumstantial evidence that the Dutch Act provided a model for the American Declaration of 1776.[33] Even if it had, the defining claim to independence could not be found in the earlier declaration. It, too, would not be known as the Dutch declaration of independence until long after its original promulgation, and in the wake of the rise to prominence of the American Declaration. It was not so-called until the 1890s. Even then, the term arose in the United States rather than in the Netherlands, during a brief burst of what has been called "Holland Mania" in which the histories of the two republics were favorably compared and the origins of many American institutions, such as freedom of religion and freedom of the press, were traced back to their alleged Dutch roots.[34] These belated baptisms of historic documents as declarations of independence indicated the increasing prestige and prominence of the American Declaration in world history rather than any genuinely long or distinguished pedigree for it.

The lack of precise generic precedents for the Declaration in 1776 should not be taken as a sign that Congress had ignored the lessons of history or the wider global context when justifying the admission of the United States to the international community. Both sides of the debate on Lee's resolution in June and July 1776 amply considered such lessons in the service of arguments for and against declaring independence.[35] The opponents of a declaration argued that neither France nor Spain would be likely to ally with the colonists out of fear that a rising power would threaten their own possessions in the Americas. Even more alarming, such a fear might impel the French and Spanish courts to ally with Britain, which "would agree to a partition of our territories, restoring Canada to France, & the Floridas to Spain, to accomplish for themselves the recovery of these colonies" that had been ceded to Britain at the end of the Seven Years' War in 1763.[36]

In the aftermath of the war, and in light of other recent international events, the threat of partition was immediate and real to many colonists. Thus in Congress on July 1, 1776, John Dickinson warned: "A *Partition* of these Colonies will take Place if G.B. cant conquer us"; this would be like "Destroying a House before We have got another. In Winter with a small Family."[37] Even after the Declaration had been declared, another Pennsylvania delegate, Benjamin Rush, feared that it would only excite Britain to greater military exertions in concert with predatory European allies. "What do you think of the States of America being divided between two or three foreign States & of seeing the Armies of two or three of the most powerful Nations in Europe upon our Coasts?" he asked on July 23, 1776.[38]

European diplomatic practice gave grounds for such fears. In 1768, the Genoese had invited France to suppress the revolt on the Mediterranean island of Corsica that had been led since 1765 by Pascal Paoli, a heroic figure whose plight was well known to, and much celebrated by, American colonists.[39] (The town of Paoli, in Pennsylvania, is still a reminder of colonial enthusiasm for the cause of Corsican independence.) In 1772 Prussia, Russia, and Austria had begun the dismemberment of Europe's largest state in the first Partition of Poland, a series of events that the colonists also followed with interest and anxiety.[40]

With these troubling precedents in mind, Daniel Leonard warned in 1775 that Britain might ally with France and Spain so that "the whole continent would become their easy prey, and would be parcelled out, Poland like," while Richard Henry Lee

speculated in April 1776 that "a slight attention to the late proceedings of many European Courts will sufficiently evince the
spirit of partition, and the assumed right of disposing of Men &
Countries like live stock on a farm that distinguishes this corrupt age. . . . Corsica, & Poland indisputably prove this."[41] A
year later, in April 1777, Thomas Paine confirmed the salience
of this fear in the discussions leading to the Declaration: "There
were reasons to believe that Britain would endeavour to make a
European matter of it." He, too, cited Corsica and Poland as
proof that "such traffics have been common in the old world."
"All Europe," he concluded, "was interested in reducing us as
rebels, and all Europe (or the greatest part at least) is interested in supporting us as Independent States."[42]

Opponents of independence had counseled delay, lest secession by one "confederacy" of colonies or another should encourage European powers to descend upon the enfeebled colonies. Congressional proponents of independence answered this
charge with another appeal to history. Unanimity could not be
achieved immediately, but "the history of the Dutch Revolution, of whom three states only confederated at first[,] proved
that a secession of some colonies would not be so dangerous as
some apprehended."[43]

The Dutch Revolt had been the first successful secession of a
province from an imperial monarchy in modern European history. The colonists were well aware of this precedent, which

had led to the creation of a federation of free states like their own.[44] As Abigail Adams wrote in April 1781, after the United Provinces had declared for the American cause, "if the old Batavian Spirit still exists among them, Britain will Rue the Day that in Breach of the Laws of Nations, she fell upon their defenceless dominions, and drew upon her . . . the combined force of all the Neutral powers." She argued that the similarities between their two causes "will cement an indissoluble bond of union between the united States of America and the united Provinces who from a similarity of circumstances have each arrived at Independance disdaining the Bondage and oppression of a Philip and a G[e]orge."[45] John Adams wrote in similar vein to the Dutch States General in the same month: "The Origins of the two Republicks are so much alike, that the History of the one seems but a Transcript from that of the other."[46] In light of the frequent comparisons drawn between the two federations, it may be significant that in the seventeenth and eighteenth centuries the United Provinces were sometimes called in English "the united states." Thus the volume of treaties Congress used when drafting the Model Treaty included an Anglo-Spanish agreement of 1667 that referred in just this way to "the united states of the Low Countries."[47]

Supporters of independence buttressed their arguments from history with more immediate assurances about the state of international affairs. Without a declaration, they reiterated, it would be "inconsistent with European delicacy for European powers to treat with us or even to receive an Ambassador from us." France and Spain had more to fear from a British victory in America, and a consequent resurgence of British power, than they did the rising power of the colonies alone. More practical considerations dictated immediate action, as "it is necessary to lose no time in opening a trade for our people, who will want clothes, and will want money too for the payment of taxes."[48]

During the debate in Congress on July 1, John Dickinson made last-ditch arguments opposing a declaration of independence, and warned against any general manifesto because "foreign Powers will not rely on Words." He recommended instead private negotiations with European powers (especially France): "We must not talk generally of foreign Powers but of those We expect to favor Us."[49] Envoys had already been sent to Europe, however, and congressional sentiment was now overwhelmingly in favor of independence. Lee's resolution passed on July 2 without any dissent, thanks to the Pennsylvania delegation, who, along with South Carolina and the formerly divided Delaware delegation, changed their votes.[50] On July 3, John Adams still lamented that the affirmation of independence had been delayed so long ("We might before this Hour, have formed Alliances with foreign States.—We should have mastered Quebec and been in possession of Canada"), but he rejoiced that it had come at last: "The Second Day of July 1776, will be the most memorable Epocha, in the History of America" and "ought to be commemorated, as the Day of Deliverance . . . from one End of this Continent to the other from this Time forward forever more."[51]

Posterity would judge that Adams had chosen not only the wrong day but also the wrong document as the focus for commemorating American independence. At the time, Adams's choice was more defensible because it acknowledged the pivotal importance of Lee's resolution as marking the point of no return. The Declaration in which the resolution would be justified to the opinions of mankind was strictly a secondary document.

Ratification of the Declaration was preceded by three days of intense debate in Congress about the wording of its text. Three weeks prior to July 4 Congress had appointed a committee consisting of Thomas Jefferson, John Adams, Benjamin Franklin, Roger Sherman, and Robert R. Livingston to draft the Declaration.[52] On June 28 Jefferson reported the fruits of the committee's work to Congress, but the draft Declaration was set aside until after the vote on Lee's resolution.

The text Jefferson submitted was written under immense pressure of congressional business, with the advice of the other members of the committee. He had constructed it in part from a series of other relevant materials: the preamble he had written for the Virginia Constitution; George Mason's Virginia

Declaration of Rights; and Lee's resolution for independence it-self. The product was a remarkable piece of textual bricolage. In form it was both a declaration—in the sense that the "Decla-ration . . . [on] Taking Up Arms" had also been a declaration—and a manifesto, that is, a detailed presentation of evidence to support "an appeal to the tribunal of the world," as Jefferson would call it in 1825. The heart of that manifesto was the list of charges that constituted "The History of the King of Great-Britain," much of which Jefferson had drawn from his Virginia preamble.[53]

Jefferson's recounting of this "History of repeated Injuries and Usurpations, all having in direct Object the Establishment of an absolute Tyranny over these States," was the culmination of a theory of conspiracy that had unfolded across Congress's state papers since 1774. The address "To the Inhabitants of the Colonies" (October 1774) had enumerated all the legislative and other designs against the colonies since "the conclusion of the late war"—that is, the Seven Years' War—in 1763. The ev-idence it presented proved, to Congress's satisfaction, "that a resolution is formed and now is carrying into execution, to ex-tinguish the freedom of these colonies, by subjecting them to a despotic government."[54]

Congress rendered its account of an unfolding global con-spiracy—because empire-wide in scale—to audiences beyond the thirteen colonies. It had informed the inhabitants of Québec in October 1774 that "the substance of the whole, divested of its smooth words, is that the Crown and its Ministers shall be as absolute throughout your extended province, as the despots of Asia or Africa." The following year it described to the Jamaica Assembly an even more comprehensive and "deliberate plan to destroy, in every part of the empire, the free constitution, for which Britain has been so long and so justly famed":

> In the East-Indies, where the effeminacy of the inhabitants promised an easy conquest, they thought it unnecessary to veil their tyrannic principles under the thinnest disguise. . . . In Britain, where the maxims of freedom were still known, but where luxury and dissipation had diminished the wonted reverence for them, the attack had been carried on in a more secret and indirect manner: Corruption has been employed to undermine them. The Americans are not enervated by effeminacy, like the inhabitants of India; nor debauched by luxury, like those of Great-Britain: It was therefore judged improper to assail them by bribery, or by undisguised force.

For these reasons, Congress informed the people of Ireland in an "Address" in July 1775, "the important contest, into which we have been driven, is now become interesting to every European state, and particularly affects the members of the British Empire."[55]

Each side in the American conflict had accused the other of such conspiratorial designs, whether for tyranny, as the Americans argued, or for independence, as Britons countered, but only the Americans projected their suspicions onto a global screen.[56] They did so, in part, to garner support from other quarters of the empire: if the American colonies should succumb to ministerial or royal despotism, then who would ever be safe from British tyranny? However, they could not have assumed their accusations would persuade the Québécois or the Irish if they had lacked any wider resonance.

Since the mid-seventeenth century, English and later British political discourse traditionally presented the freedoms of Northern Europe and its American colonies as hardwon, persistently embattled, and perpetually on the defensive in a world populated mostly by slaves ruled over by despots and tyrants. "Liberty is the natural birthright of mankind," exclaimed the English political economist Arthur Young in 1772; "and yet to take a comprehensive view of the world, how few enjoy it!" He calculated that only 33.5 million people out of an estimated global population of 775.3 million were not "the miserable slaves of despotic tyrants . . . and of these few so large a portion as 12,500,000 are subjects of the British empire."[57]

The most eloquent statement of this view had come in Paine's *Common Sense,* when he concluded his account of the injuries visited on the Americans with these rousing lines:

> O ye that love mankind! Ye that dare oppose not only the tyranny, but the tyrant, stand forth! Every spot of the old world is over-run with oppression. Freedom hath been hunted around the Globe. Asia and Africa have long expelled her:——Europe regards her like a stranger, and England hath given her warning to depart. O! receive the fugitive, and prepare in time an asylum for mankind.[58]

Five months later, the authors of the Declaration would share Paine's judgment that the king was to blame for the designs against his American subjects. But they did not imitate Paine's apocalyptic rhetoric, focusing only on those details in his global panorama of encroaching tyranny that applied specifically to the American colonies.

The Declaration's central catalogue of the king's "Injuries and Usurpations" was deliberately unspecific regarding places and dates. Any of the multiple charges arrayed against the monarch could apply to any, or all, of the colonies.[59] Few of those charges would have been entirely new to anyone who had been following the American pamphlet wars of 1774–1776 at all closely: for example, many of them had appeared in Congress's letter to the inhabitants of the colonies in 1774 and in Jefferson's *Summary View of the Rights of British America* that same year.[60] In the *Summary View,* Jefferson had listed them in the context of an address to the king himself from the Virginia House of Burgesses and in support of a federal conception in which the king was but the "chief magistrate of the British empire" composed of multiple "states," "the distinct and independent governments" of British America among them. The "bold succession of injuries" that Jefferson described was laid at Parliament's door, not the king's, to "plainly prove a deliberate and systematical plan of reducing us to slavery."[61]

By contrast, the Declaration's litany of abuses began with a series of general offenses against the colonies, then followed with a set of more specific charges that the king had assented to acts of legislation "to subject us to a Jurisdiction foreign to our Constitution," before culminating in a list of more wide-ranging physical and economic assaults on the inhabitants of the colonies.[62] The first group comprised charges that the king had directly interfered in colonial affairs by blocking colonial legislation, disrupting colonial assemblies, discouraging immigration, interfering with the judicial process and judicial freedom, and imposing a standing army on the colonies. The second group specified the metropolitan legislation that had been passed without regard to the needs of the colonies, including "cutting off our Trade with all Parts of the World," "transporting us beyond the Seas to be tried for pretended Offences," and "abolishing the free System of English Laws in a neighbouring Province" (that is, Québec).

As the charges mounted rhetorically to their crescendo, so the third, and climactic, group moved outward from the purview of domestic administration and colonial legislation into the realm of the law of nations. The king, the Declaration charged, "has plundered our Seas, ravaged our Coasts, burnt our Towns, and destroyed the Lives of our People." He was importing foreign mercenaries to complete "the Works of Death, Desolation and Tyranny, already begun with circumstances of Cruelty and Perfidy scarcely paralleled in the most barbarous Ages, and totally unworthy the Head of a civilized Nation." He had forced "our fellow Citizens taken Captive on the high Seas" to take up arms against their own countrymen, and, in the crowning evidence of his despotism, "He has excited domestic Insurrections amongst us, and has endeavoured to bring on the Inhabitants of our Frontiers, the merciless Indian Savages, whose known Rule of Warfare, is an undistinguished Destruction of all Ages, Sexes, and Conditions."

The British people provided no defense against these depredations because they would not "disavow these Usurpations, which, would inevitably interrupt our Connections and Correspondence"—that is, would cut off the colonies from all kinds of commerce with the wider world. There was thus no alternative to suspending the previous familial bonds between Britons and British Americans and replacing them with the relations of independent peoples under the law of nations: "We must, therefore, acquiesce in the Necessity which denounces our Separation, and hold them, as we hold the rest of Mankind, Enemies in War, in Peace, Friends."

In the version of the Declaration ultimately ratified by Congress and published to the world, the rhetorical climax of the long train of alleged abuses was the accusations that George III had attempted to stir up "domestic insurrections"—that is, slave rebellions like those the British governor Dunmore had encouraged by proclamation in Virginia in 1775 to undermine the colony's plantation economy—and had drawn "the merciless Indian Savages" down upon the colonists.[63]

These charges implied that the king had effectively placed the colonies "beyond the line" of civilized practice in warfare. The customary law of European nations in the eighteenth century formally excluded such incursions from the pale of civilized behavior. The Declaration implied that to readmit illicit violence and savagery—in the form of freed slaves and indigenous modes of warfare—within the bounds of the colonies themselves was an affront to an emerging international order and not just to the sensibilities of particular colonists. Such a charge could of course easily be turned around, as the British demonstrated during the American War when they similarly accused the colonists of engaging in savage practices contrary to the prevailing European laws of war.[64]

In Jefferson's original draft of the Declaration, the final charge against the king made an even more explicit appeal to the law of nations and to the norms of contemporary European civilization. George III, Jefferson contended,

> has waged cruel war against human nature itself, violating it's most sacred rights of life & liberty in the persons of a distant people who never offended him, captivating & carrying them into slavery in another hemisphere, or to incur miserable death in their transportation thither. this piratical warfare, the opprobrium of *infidel* powers, is the warfare of the CHRISTIAN king of Great Britain . . . and that this assemblage of horrors might want no fact of distinguished die, he is now exciting those very people to rise in arms among us, and to purchase that liberty of which *he* deprived them, by murdering the people upon whom *he* also has obtruded them; thus paying off former crimes committed against the *liberties* of one people, with crimes which he urges them to commit against the *lives* of another.

This passage seems doubly anomalous, both because Jefferson himself was embroiled in the institution of slavery and because these words would inevitably be excised from the final version of the Declaration by the representatives of those states that wished to continue the slave trade or had been implicated in it before 1776. As Jefferson reported, "the clause . . . reprobating the enslaving the inhabitants of Africa, was struck out in complaisance to South Carolina and Georgia . . . our Northern brethren also I believe felt a little tender under those censures; for tho' their people have very few slaves themselves yet they have been pretty considerable carriers of them to others."[65] Nonetheless, in the context of Jefferson's original draft of the Declaration, the passage marked the logical climax to the train of abuses with which the king had been charged.[66]

However implausible it may have been to lay personal responsibility for the slave trade on the shoulders of George III, the comparison between "the CHRISTIAN king of Great Britain" and "*infidel* Powers" like those of Morocco and Algiers who engaged in "piratical warfare" against Europeans, outside the norms of the law of nations, recalled the charge in the *Summary View* that the king had "preferr[ed] the immediate advantages of a few British corsairs to the lasting interests of the American states, and to the rights of human nature, deeply wounded by this infamous practice," by refusing to countenance the abolition of the slave trade.[67]

It also hinted at one of the most troubling implications of American independence: that the Royal Navy would no longer

protect American shipping from assaults by the Barbary corsairs who preyed on merchant vessels in the Mediterranean.
When the United States entered into its first defensive alliance,
with France in February 1778, the provisions of the Franco-
American Treaty of Amity and Commerce included the crucial
clause offering French protection for "the Benefit, Conveniency
and Safety of the said United States, and each of them, their
Subjects, People, and Inhabitants, and their Vessels and Effects,
against all Violence, Insult, Attacks, or Depredations on the
Part of the . . . Princes and States of Barbary, or their Subjects."[68]

The longest passage that Congress excised from the Declaration was inflammatory not least because Jefferson had rendered
equivalent both the free inhabitants of British America and the
enslaved by calling each a "people." In the opening paragraph of
his original draft, Jefferson had written, "When in the course
of human events it becomes necessary for *a people* to advance
from that subordination in which they have hitherto remained,"
which Congress amended to become the more familiar, "When
in the Course of human Events, it becomes necessary for *One
people* to dissolve the Political Bands which have connected
them *with another*" (my emphases). In the Declaration adopted
by Congress, Britons and Americans alone were called "peoples" in two mutually reinforcing senses: as the inhabitants of
two territories constituted politically as sovereign bodies, and

also as two of the units within the traditional law of nations, or what legally minded contemporaries would have called the law of peoples (what in Roman law had been called the *jus gentium* and what, in contemporary French and German legal language, was called the *droit des gens* or *Völkerrecht)*. The excision of the passage relating to the slave trade and the alteration of the opening sentence of the Declaration removed any such parity between Africans and Americans, as "peoples" or as the victims of "subordination."[69] Yet these would be just the terms in which Jefferson would later argue for emancipation in *Notes on the State of Virginia* (1785): the Virginia legislature could free the enslaved by sending them to colonize the western lands, with a duty on the Virginians "to declare them a free and independant people, and to extend to them our alliance and protection."[70]

The wider world imagined in the Declaration—both in its drafts and in its final published version—was a world of peoples linked by both benign and malign forms of commerce. It was also an arena of warfare between Americans and Britons, as well as among their various allies and enemies. This international community was populated mostly by mutually recognizing sovereign states, but it was threatened by outlaw powers who acted more like pirates, those traditional enemies of humankind engaged in warfare against humanity itself.[71] In many ways this was a recognizably modern world, in which commerce and war are the most conspicuous forms of interaction between different peoples and states. Even among European thinkers, that conception of the interactions between states was barely a century old in 1776.[72] Yet it was also a world in which metaphysical norms—"the Laws of Nature and of Nature's God"—could still be appealed to, alongside the "known Rules of Warfare" and cultural standards like civility and barbarism.

This was the world into which the members of Congress believed they were introducing the United States of America by means of the Declaration of Independence. In its self-justifying pamphlet *Observations on the American Revolution* (1779), Congress took independence to be a settled but embattled fact: "we must hold ourselves ready to repel force by force wherever assailed, and firmly retort to every infringement of the law of nations with unfailing perseverance." If the independence of the United States could be defended, and the law of nations upheld, then the United States would become what Thomas Paine and others had predicted: an asylum for oppressed humanity, a beacon of knowledge and benevolence, and a universal entrepôt for the commerce of the world.[73]

This would also be the millennialist vision Ezra Stiles, the Congregationalist preacher and president of Yale College, promised in the immediate aftermath of British recognition of American independence in 1783:

This great American revolution, this recent political phenomenon of a new sovereignty arising among the sovereign powers of the earth, will be attended to and contem-
plated by all nations. Navigation will carry the American
flag around the globe itself; and display the Thirteen Stripes
and New Constellation at *Bengal* and *Canton,* on the *Indus*
and the *Ganges,* on the *Whang-ho* and the *Yang-tse-kiang . . .*
knowledge will be brought home and treasured to *America;*
and being here digested and carried to the highest perfection, may reblaze back from *America* to *Europe, Asia* and *Africa,* and illumine the world with TRUTH and LIBERTY.

As Stiles noted in the second edition of his sermon, *The United
States Elevated to Glory and Honour,* published two years later
in 1785, this vision was already becoming a reality, with the
return to the United States of the first American East-India
ships from Canton, Macao, and Calcutta.[74] The Declaration had
imagined a new world only for the pursuit of American sovereignty. Now, its consequences would shape that world, thanks
to the "new sovereignty . . . among the sovereign powers of the
earth" that it had helped to bring into being.

CHAPTER TWO

The Declaration of Independence in the World

In the early decades after 1776, the Declaration inspired more attention and commentary outside the United States than it did at home. Little of that attention was directed toward the Declaration's second paragraph; indeed, most of it either dealt with refuting the grievances against King George III or reflected more broadly on the implications of American independence for the emerging international order of the late eighteenth-century Atlantic world.

Partisan strife at home, and debate about the nature of independence abroad, made it necessary for Americans to rehabilitate their Declaration after 1815. A document that had addressed itself to the "Opinions of Mankind" and to "a candid

World" had to be recovered from its cosmopolitan contexts and made into something specifically American. This effort of domestication would have two equal and opposite effects: first, it would hide from Americans the original meaning of the Declaration as an international, and even a global, document; second, it would ensure that within the United States only proponents of slavery, supporters of Southern secession, and anti-individualist critics of rights talk would be able to recall that original meaning.

The very fact of American independence in the eyes of the world confirmed the effects of this change in the document's meaning for Americans. As Woodrow Wilson noted on July 4, 1914, in a speech at Independence Hall in Philadelphia, "In one sense, the Declaration of Independence has lost its significance. It has lost its significance as a declaration of national independence. . . . now nobody anywhere would dare doubt that we are independent and can maintain our independence. As a declaration of independence, therefore, it is a mere historic document."[1]

The primary intention behind the Declaration of Independence in 1776 had been to affirm before world opinion the rights of one people organized into thirteen states to enter the international arena on a footing equal to other, similar states. The authors of the Declaration had sought the admission of the United States of America to a pre-existing international order;

accordingly, they had couched their appeal to the powers of the earth in terms that those powers would understand and, Congress hoped, also approve. "In our Transactions with European States, it is certainly of Importance neither to transgress, nor to fall short of those Maxims, by which they regulate their Conduct towards one another," explained James Wilson in January 1777.[2] In this sense, the Declaration signaled to the world that the Americans intended their revolution to be decidedly *un*-revolutionary. It would affirm the maxims of European statecraft, not affront them. It would conform as far as possible to the regulatory norms of contemporary politics. Least of all would it be an incitement to rebellion or revolution elsewhere in the world, rather than an inducement to reform.[3]

The Declaration of Independence has been called "a document performed in the discourse of the *jus gentium* [the law of nations] rather than *jus civile* [the civil law]."[4] Owing to its success in securing American independence, this fact has generally been overlooked. The document's opening and closing statements have been taken for granted because in retrospect they seemed to have enduringly confirmed that independence. Yet they are, after all, the most prominent sentences in the document, the statements of what the United States intended to become: "to assume among the Powers of the Earth, the separate and equal Station to which the Laws of Nature and of Nature's God entitle them"; and of what they could do once they had achieved that goal: "to levy War, conclude Peace, contract Alliances, establish Commerce, and to do all other Acts and Things which INDEPENDENT STATES may of right do." The rest of the Declaration provided only a statement of the abstract principles upon which the assertion of such standing within the international order rested, and an accounting of the grievances that had compelled the United States to assume their independent station among "the Powers of the Earth."

Though largely forgotten now, this understanding of the Declaration's meaning held sway even among American commentators for almost half a century after 1776. Thus John Adams, writing in 1781, called the Declaration "that memorable Act, by which [the United States] assumed an equal Station among the Nations." For a group of Americans in Paris, writing to Thomas Jefferson on July 4, 1789, the document was "that declaratory act which announced to the world the existence of an empire." To David Ramsay, in his *History of the American Revolution* (1789), it was "the act of the united colonies for separating themselves from the government of Great-Britain, and declaring their independence." For John Quincy Adams, speaking on Independence Day, 1821, "the Declaration of Independence, in its primary import, was merely an *occasional* state-paper. It was a solemn exposition to the world, of the *causes* which had *compelled* the people of a small portion of the British empire, to cast off their allegiance and renounce the protection of the

British king: and to dissolve their social connexion with the British people." From the other side of the sectional divide, John C. Calhoun concurred some years later: "The act was, in fact, but a formal and solemn announcement to the world, that the colonies had ceased to be dependent communities, and had become free and independent States."[5]

This emphasis on the state-making capacity of the Declaration was partly an American response to a counter-revolutionary critique of theories of natural rights in the 1770s that foreshadowed the much more vehement offensive against the French Declarations of the Rights of Man and of the Citizen in the 1790s. The French Revolution would cast other shadows across the cause of American independence. The claim of some French revolutionaries that their movement owed its inspiration to the United States rendered key documents like the Declaration suspect and dangerous in the eyes of those who feared the wholesale destruction of the political and diplomatic order of the Atlantic world. Though it is now common to assimilate the American and French Revolutions to each other, and to include both in a broader "Age of the Democratic Revolution" or "Age of Revolutions," such an identification obscures major differences between the two political movements when considered in their international context.[6]

International affairs were a major determinant even of the domestic, American, meaning of the Declaration. The elevation of the Declaration to the status of "American scripture," and the centrality of its second paragraph to that sanctified position, could take place only once all doubt had been laid to rest that the American and French Revolutions were but two distinct moments in a single movement against the established order. In the words of the German counter-revolutionary writer Friedrich Gentz—translated for an American audience by John Quincy Adams in 1800—"The American revolution was from beginning to end, on the part of the Americans, merely a *defensive revolution;* the French was from beginning to end, in the highest sense of the word, *an offensive revolution.*" It was regrettable, Gentz thought, that the Americans had with an "empty pomp of words" claimed the possession of natural and inalienable rights in the Declaration, but fortunately, "they allowed these speculative ideas no visible influence upon their practical measures and resolves." Theirs was a legal revolution, directed against specific oppressive measures and not against monarchical principles *tout court.* On these grounds, "there was, *in itself,* nothing unnatural, nothing revolting, nothing plainly irreconcilable with the maxims of the law of nations, and the laws of self-preservation, in the alliance, which France contracted with them."[7]

The maxims of the law of nations themselves were changing in the late eighteenth century, and with them, the interpretation of the Declaration as a document of international law. It was in this period that "the law of nations, long and inextricably associated with the law of nature came . . . to be understood as positive law, made by sovereign states, acting collectively through authorized means, for their progressively more complex ends."[8] As one contemporary commentator remarked, it was "hardly possible that the simple law of nature should be sufficient, even between individuals, and still less between nations, when they come to frequent and carry on commerce with each other." States had to temper the law of nature in practice and by consent: "The whole of the rights and obligations thus established between two nations, form the positive law of nations between them. It is called *positive,* particular, or arbitrary, in opposition to natural, universal and necessary law."[9] Thomas Jefferson himself encapsulated the prevailing wisdom of the period when he stated in 1793 that "the Law of Nations . . . is composed of three branches. 1. the Moral law of our nature. 2. the Usages of nations. 3. their special Conventions."[10] These overlapping conceptions of the law of nations would decisively shape the reception of the Declaration outside the United States in the decades immediately after 1776.

Reports of American independence traveled immediately across the Atlantic Ocean and then deep into Continental Europe in the summer and autumn of 1776. Only two months after Congress had passed its resolution on July 2, word of independence had reached as far east as Warsaw.[11] The itinerary of the news illustrated the remarkable speed of communications in the late eighteenth century, as well as the richly developed network of newspapers and journals, and of spies and agents, that relied on the transmission of such information. Word had spread first to London, and from there to Scotland, Ireland, and Holland, before it was carried to the German lands, Scandinavia, and Southern and Eastern Europe, all in the space of barely eight weeks.

The text of the Declaration of Independence first appeared in London newspapers in the second week of August 1776.[12] Less than a week later, it was printed in Edinburgh, where the philosopher and historian (and strong supporter of American independence) David Hume could have read it on August 20, only five days before his death on August 25; it also appeared in the Dublin press on August 24.[13] The next week it was reported in Madrid on August 27, and the Dutch press—beginning with the widely distributed *Gazette de Leyde* from Leiden—picked it up on August 30; the following day it also appeared in Vienna.[14] By September 2, a Danish newspaper in Copenhagen carried a translation of the Declaration on its front page. On September 14 readers learned of it in Florence. The following month, a complete German translation was published in a Swiss journal in Basel.[15]

Despite this initially rapid transmission through the channels of late eighteenth-century print culture, the Declaration's progress was somewhat hampered by the fact that it was written in English. French, not English, was the reigning language of diplomacy, and English was not yet a major lingua franca even for the learned across Europe and the Americas.[16] The worldwide community of English speakers would have amounted to barely more than the 12.5 million "subjects of the British empire" Arthur Young had estimated in 1772: that is, roughly the population of Austria (over 15 million), fewer than the inhabitants of Russia (circa 19 million), more than half the contemporary population of France (24 million), perhaps half the number of the Ottoman sultan's 28–30 million subjects, but only a fraction of the nearly 270 million inhabitants of the Qing empire in 1776.[17]

Though English would not greatly aid the spread of the Declaration, American independence would in due course help to secure the global dominance of English. John Adams predicted in 1780 that "English is destined to be in the next and succeeding centuries more generally the language of the world than Latin was in the last or French is in the present age."[18] (In this regard, it is notable that the Declaration seems never to have been translated into Latin, in 1776 or since.) Two years later, Caleb Whitefoord, the Scottish secretary to the British peace commissioners in Paris, concurred when replying to a French taunt that "the United States would form the greatest empire in the world": "Yes, sir, and they will *all* speak English; every one of them."[19] Not quite every one within the United States spoke English, of course. The colonies contained a diverse ethnic mix of Dutch, Germans, French, and Africans, as well as Britons and Irish. Indeed, the very first translations of the Declaration, into German, appeared between July 6 and 9, 1776, as a broadside and then in a Philadelphia newspaper, for the benefit of the local German community.[20]

In the second half of 1776, the Declaration itself received little or no direct commentary in France, Italy, Germany, Poland, Switzerland, or Spain. The immediate effect of the less specific news of independence on Europe was minimal.[21] Only in England and Ireland did it have any direct political consequences. Supporters of the British cause had predicted that "the Declaration for an Independency must totally silence any Advocates [the Americans] had in England."[22] Some of the firmer partisans of the American cause may have been cheered by the news. Wavering sympathizers of the Americans recoiled as Congress had clearly marked a point of no return in the conflict with Britain.[23] Edmund Burke, for one, later histrionically confessed that "the day that he first heard of the American states having claimed Independency, it made him sick at heart; it struck him to his soul, because he saw it was a claim essentially injurious to this country, and a claim which Great Britain could never get rid of. Never! Never! Never!"[24]

British and American Loyalist opponents of the American rebellion either deplored the presumptuousness of the colonists or took comfort from the fact that a long-meditated conspiracy for independence had at last been flushed out into the open. On Staten Island with the British forces, Ambrose Serle, the secretary to the British admiral Lord Richard Howe, expressed his horror at the Declaration on July 13, 1776: "A more impudent, false and atrocious Proclamation was never fabricated by the Hands of Man."[25] Howe himself sent one of the first copies of the Declaration back to London in August 1776. He also recognized how it had changed relations between the British and the colonists when he met a congressional delegation, comprising John Adams, Benjamin Franklin, and Edward Rutledge, on Staten Island in September 1776: "They themselves had changed the ground . . . by their Declaration of Independency, which, if it could not be got over, precluded him from all Treaty . . . he had not, nor did he expect to have, Powers to consider the Colonies in the light of Independent States."[26]

The most efficient transmitters of the Declaration across the Atlantic were not the agents of Congress but British civilian and military officials in North America. During the autumn of 1776, these officers sent five copies of the Declaration back to Britain, where they later found their way into the British state papers. These copies now make up the largest collection of original printings of the document outside the United States.[27]

At the time, they seem to have aroused no immediate ministerial reaction. What that reaction might have been can be inferred from the response of the exiled former governor of Massachusetts, Thomas Hutchinson, who was in London just as details of the Declaration arrived: "The Congress has issued a most infamous Paper reciting a great number of Pretended tyrannical deeds of the King and declaring their Independence."[28] In a delicious irony, Hutchinson had received an honorary degree from Oxford, the most conservative of contemporary British universities, on July 4, 1776. Within a few weeks of hearing of the Declaration, he also published one of only two British pamphlets in reply to it: as well he might have done, for he was the intended target of some of its most egregious charges.[29] Hutchinson surely shared the sentiments of George III, who delivered a speech to the British Parliament on October 31, 1776, in which he condemned the "daring and desperate" spirit of the leaders of his American colonies, who had "presumed to set up their rebellious confederacies for independent states."[30]

On the western side of the Atlantic, silencing the Declaration was a more effective governmental response to its challenge than attempting to refute it. When word of the Declaration had reached the British colony of Nova Scotia, in August 1776, the British governor allowed only the last paragraph of the document to be printed, lest the rest of it "gain over to them (the Rebels) many converts, and inflame the minds of his Majesty's loyal and faithful subjects of the Province of *Nova Scotia*."[31] Back in Britain, however, the government could not respond openly and officially to the Declaration, for that "would be to recognise that equality and independence, to which subjects, persisting in revolt, cannot fail to pretend . . . This would be to recognise the right of other states to interfere in matters, from which all foreign interposition should for ever be precluded."[32] Lord North's ministry did, however, secretly commission a rebuttal to the Declaration, from which these words are taken. The author of *Answer to the Declaration of the American Congress* (1776) was John Lind, a young lawyer and pamphleteer who had previously come to the administration's notice with his pamphlets *Remarks on the Principal Acts of the Thirteenth Parliament* (1775) and *Three Letters to Dr Price, Containing Remarks on his Observations on the Nature of Civil Liberty, the Principles of Government, and the Justice and Policy of the War with America* (1776).[33]

Two versions of *Answer to the Declaration* appeared in 1776. The ministry seems to have judged that the first version went too far both in trying to imagine the justifications the Americans might have had for issuing their Declaration and in presuming to offer the "Outlines of a Counter-Declaration" that the king could present in refutation of the Americans' assertions. The ministry suppressed the initial text of the *Answer*—only one copy of which now survives—and had the whole work revised before eight thousand copies were issued in multiple editions over the course of 1776.[34] Five hundred copies of this revised *Answer to the Declaration* were sent from London to America, to instruct the British forces and to rebut American arguments in favor of independence.[35]

The *Answer to the Declaration* was mostly a point-by-point examination and refutation of the charges against the king. Lind denied that the Americans were still anything other than treacherous individuals, rather than states, and hence argued that they were still rebels rather than legitimate corporate belligerents. To do otherwise would have been to make a mockery of the idea of allegiance, let alone legality; after all, if the colonists were acknowledged to be independent citizens of a foreign state, what could have prevented a pirate like Captain Kidd from protecting himself against criminal prosecution by declaring himself independent? "Instead of the guilty pirate," Lind warned, "he would have become the *independent* prince; and taken among the *'maritime'* powers—*'that separate and equal station, to which'*—he too might have discovered—*'the laws of nature and of nature's God entitled him.'"*

Finally, Lind mocked the colonists for their hypocrisy in announcing the natural equality of all mankind while failing to free their slaves: such rights were hardly inalienable, and clearly not natural, if they were denied to "these wretched beings."[36] Thomas Hutchinson similarly wished "to ask the Delegates of

Maryland, Virginia, and the Carolinas, how their Constituents justify the depriving more than an hundred thousand Africans of their rights to liberty, and *the pursuit of happiness,* and in some degree, to their lives, if their rights are so absolutely unalienable." The English abolitionist Thomas Day, writing in 1776, went even further in his criticism: "If there be an object truly ridiculous in nature, it is an American patriot, signing resolutions of independency with the one hand, and with the other brandishing a whip over his affrighted slaves."[37]

The *Answer to the Declaration* was one of only a handful of contemporary publications to comment on the natural rights claims of the Declaration's second paragraph. Among Continental writers, the French duc de La Rochefoucauld d'Enville alone, writing in the guise of a banker in London, considered the claim that all men are created equal to be an established truth in all religions. He saw nothing in the Declaration's further rights claims that could be construed as a challenge to general rights of sovereignty. This was of a piece with his effusive assessment that the Declaration was "the greatest event of the campaign, of the war itself, and perhaps of this century."[38] Among British and Loyalist respondents, only Hutchinson dealt with the question of rights, and even then he did so briefly and dismissively, while a letter in the August 1776 issue of *The Scots Magazine* reduced the Declaration's self-evident truths to absurdity: "these gentry assume to themselves an unalienable right of talking nonsense."[39] Two years later in 1778, in the course of versifying the whole Declaration, grievances and all, an obscure English satirist named Joseph Peart wittily mocked the American assertion

> *That all men are born free alike,*
> *And are undoubtedly allow'd,*
> *By providence to be endow'd,*
> *(As many a learned author writes)*
> *With some unalienable rights;*
> *'Mong these we lay the greatest stress,*
> *On life, pursuit of happiness,*
> *And (what is best of all the three)*
> *Of uncontrouled liberty.*
> *For surely no one can believe,*
> *But he's a certain right to live,*
> *Without receiving check or stop here,*
> *As long as ever he thinks proper.*[40]

The "Short Review of the Declaration" accompanying Lind's *Answer* similarly judged the principles upon which the Americans claimed their independence to be tautologous, redundant, inconsistent, and hypocritical. "If to what they now demand they were entitled by any law of God," thundered the reviewer, "they had only to produce that law, and all controversy was at an end. Instead of this, what do they produce? What they call self-evident truths. . . . At the same time, to secure these rights, they are content that Governments should be instituted. They perceive not, or will not seem to perceive, that nothing which can be called government ever was, or ever could be, in any instance, exercised, but at the expence of one or other of those rights" to life, liberty, or the pursuit of happiness.[41]

This precocious attack on the language of individual natural rights in the *Answer to the Declaration* was a significant contribution to late eighteenth-century counter-revolutionary discourse. The "Short Review" formed a link between the American and French Revolutions because its main author was not Lind but his friend the philosopher Jeremy Bentham.[42] Bentham had earlier collaborated on Lind's *Remarks* and had prepared a devastating (but unpublished) criticism of what he called "negative liberty" for inclusion in Lind's *Three Letters to Dr Price*.[43] Until the end of his life, Bentham remained critical of the principles that underpinned the Declaration. "Who can help lamenting that so rational a cause should be rested upon reasons, so much fitter to beget objections, than to remove them?" he complained in 1789, referring to the Virginia Declaration of Rights, the Massachusetts Declaration, and the Declaration itself; almost half a century later he still called the Virginia Declaration "a hodge-podge of confusion and absurdity, in which the thing to be proved is all along taken for granted."[44]

The basis of Bentham's criticism remained consistent. Ascribing laws to nature, and deriving natural rights from such laws, was not simply nonsense but "rhetorical nonsense, nonsense upon stilts," as he called it in his demolition of the French Declaration of the Rights of Man and the Citizen almost twenty years after his earlier reply to the Declaration of Independence.[45] Defensible rights could be derived only from the positive acts of identifiable legislators. In the relations between nations, the only positive acts were the transactions of sovereigns that made up a body of positive "international law," as Bentham had been the first to call it in 1780. His attack on the premises of the Declaration may have helped to sharpen his sense that this new term was needed to denominate an increasingly salient body of law. If the Continental Congress were to be acknowledged as a legitimate executive body, then its Declaration could be construed as a positive act within the ambit of international law. However, it could be acknowledged in this way only if the Declaration itself were recognized as the positive act that had endowed Congress with international personality as a sovereign body. How could independence be declared, except by a body that was already independent in the sense understood by the law of nations?

This would be the nub of the legal argument raised by the Declaration in the decades after 1776. A mere declaration alone could not constitute independence; it could only an-nounce what had already been achieved by other means. The Declaration had thus to perform American independence in the very act of announcing it. As the French philosopher Jacques Derrida pointed out in 1976, on the anniversary of American independence, "The question remains. How is a State made or founded, how does a State make or found itself? . . . Who signs all these authorisations to sign?"[46] Bentham had asked a similar question two centuries earlier in his *Fragment on Government* (April 1776): "When is it, in short, that a *revolt* shall be deemed to have taken place, and when . . . is it that that revolt shall be deemed to such a degree successful, as to have settled into *independence?*"[47] At this point he refused to say, but the question remained when he joined Lind's attack on the Declaration later that same year.

American independence could be accomplished only through external recognition, in the form of tangible military assistance and diplomatic and commercial transactions. Accordingly, Congress instructed its commissioners in Paris, Silas Deane, Benjamin Franklin, and Arthur Lee, "to obtain as early as possible a publick acknowledgement of the Independancy of these States of the Crown and Parliament of Great Britain by the Court of France."[48] Congress found the long silence from the French court in 1776 and for more than a year afterward particularly troubling. The first American representative in Paris, Deane, did not receive the copy of the Declaration that was sent to him on July 8, 1776, along with instructions to "immediately communicate the piece to the Court of France, and send copies of it to the other Courts of Europe. It may be well also to procure copies of it into French, and get it published in the gazettes." A second copy arrived only in November 1776, by which time the news of American independence had been circulating for at least three months elsewhere in Europe.[49]

French audiences could by then have read a translation of the Declaration in the *Gazette de Leyde* or another in the Parisian *Political and Historical Journal* dated September 10, 1776. Two more translations would appear the following year in the *Affairs of England and America*—a journal secretly sponsored by the French foreign minister, the comte de Vergennes—and other versions could be found in subsequent years in two collections of American state papers published in Paris that were associated with Benjamin Franklin, the *Collection of Constitutional Laws of the English Colonies* (1778), which was dedicated to him, and the *Constitutions of the Thirteen Colonies of the United States of America* (1783), which he revised.[50] However, though the marquis de Lafayette and others admired the Declaration, the French paid much more attention to the American state constitutions than to the Declaration itself in the years before and after 1789.[51]

When the French court did eventually enter into a treaty of alliance with the United States in February 1778, following the watershed American victory over British forces at the battle of Saratoga, it did so "to maintain effectually the liberty, Sovereignty and independence absolute and unlimited of the said United States," among other things.[52] This was, of course, what Congress had hoped for all along, having simultaneously created committees for drafting the Declaration and the Model Treaty.

France's *de facto* recognition of American independence by the treaties of 1778 elicited immediate denunciation from Britain. The ministry commissioned the historian of empire and Board of Trade member Edward Gibbon to write a "justificatory memorial" in French exposing the bad faith of the French court in making an alliance with "the dark agents of the English Colonies, who founded their pretended independence on nothing but the boldness of their revolt." Gibbon argued that the alliance was a specific repudiation of the articles of peace signed between Britain and France at the end of the Seven Years' War; it was also a general offense against the law of nations, which debarred any power from offering aid to rebels within the dominions of another legitimate sovereign. To believe otherwise would be "to introduce maxims as new as they are false and dangerous into the jurisprudence of Europe" and would lead to further revolts in the American provinces of France and Spain. The Americans themselves should also be warned that their "pretended independence, bought with so many miseries and so much blood," would soon be subject to the despotic will of a foreign court.[53]

To Gibbon's solemn admonitions and aspersions on American independence the English radical John Wilkes retorted: "Why must it be 'la déclaration *(ouverte)* de leur indépendance *(prétendue)*' . . . after the third anniversary of the *independance* of *The United States* had been celebrated? The *independance* of the country is tolerably well established, when a foreign prince cannot make an exciseman": that is, when the former ruler could no longer appoint even the lowliest administrative officers because he had long since lost effective control. American independence, Wilkes argued, was based not on the Americans' rebellious boldness but on the facts so rigorously set forth in "the famous Declaration of *Independance* of the memorable fourth of July, 1776."[54]

If the Declaration's purpose was to enable the rebellious colonies to enter into diplomatic and commercial alliances with other powers, as Paine, Richard Henry Lee, the local declarations, and the drafting committee of the Continental Congress intended, at what point did the colonies become states and the rebels acquire legitimacy? The United States formally entered the international system upon joining the Franco-American alliance; only after that could the question of American independence be treated as a positive, albeit contested, international fact.

Yet the fact of independence was one thing; the basis on which the Declaration had asserted it quite another, for only positive acts could constitute statehood. If a mere declaration was insufficient, and the acknowledgment of independence by Britain inconceivable, would recognition of independence by a third power, such as France, be necessary to ensure legitimacy? Would even recognition by third parties be inadequate until the metropolitan government had conceded independence, as Britain did only by the Peace of Paris in 1783?[55]

These questions concerning independence, statehood, and recognition were at the heart of the emerging positive law of nations in the late eighteenth century, and the Declaration— like American independence itself—was received in this light after 1783 and in Europe. These aspects of the Declaration became the focus of the rapidly evolving argument about the theory of the legal recognition of states. To claim an equal station for the United States among "the Powers of the Earth," the colonists needed more than the bare assertion that those states were entitled to their independence by virtue of the "Laws of Nature and of Nature's God." The modern exponents of natural law, such as Vattel, had argued that states did, indeed, possess a right to existence, independence, and equality. But the means by which new states might acquire that right, if they had not previously possessed it, became a central topic of international legal argument only in the late eighteenth century, partly in response to the issues of recognition raised by the Declaration of Independence itself.[56]

The Declaration became a prominent exhibit in the earliest discussion of the recognition of states. This came from the German jurist and belletrist J. C. W. von Steck in 1783. Previously, discussions of state recognition in European public law had concerned individual rulers' rights of dynastic succession. Steck's approach was original in that he treated the recognition and legitimation not just of princes but of states in general. His account accordingly focused on republics like the United Provinces and the United States. In the latter case, Steck denied that American independence had had any international standing until it was formally and positively recognized by Britain. Writing in the immediate aftermath of the Treaty of Paris, he deemed French recognition in 1778 to have been premature, and hence without constructive force, because it had not been accompanied by any British renunciation of rights.[57]

In 1789 the Göttingen law professor G. F. von Martens pressed Steck's point further to argue that, "when once obedience has been formally refused, and the refusing party has entered into the possession of the independence demanded, the dispute becomes the same as those which happen between independent states," subject, however, to the major proviso that the offended party could rightfully construe any aid or succor offered to the newly independent state as an act of war: "The conduct that Great Britain observed . . . after the Colonies of North America declared themselves independent, may serve to illustrate this subject."[58] Some fifty years later, the question of state recognition raised by American independence had become canonized as one of the great *causes célèbres* of modern international law as it passed decisively into its positivist phase.[59]

The victory of the Americans in their war of independence against Britain changed the status of the Declaration outside the United States. Britain's recognition of American independence in 1783 by Article I of the Peace of Paris indisputably confirmed what the Declaration had contentiously affirmed in 1776: "His *Britannick* Majesty acknowledges the said *United States* . . . to be Free, Sovereign, and Independent States" *de jure,* and no longer just *de facto.*[60] The momentousness of that event was not lost on Edmund Burke: "A great revolution has happened—a revolution made, not by chopping and changing of power in any one of the existing states, but by the appearance of a new state, of a new species, in a new part of the globe. It has made as great a change in all the relations, and balances, and gravitation of power, as the appearance of a new planet would in the system of the solar world."[61] Once the Declaration's immediate purpose had been served, the opening and closing paragraphs fell into oblivion. As a sympathetic foreign observer, the marquis de Condorcet, noted in 1786, in France

American "independence is recognized and assured; [our politicians] seem to regard it with indifference."[62] Because American independence was now an acknowledged fact in international politics, there was little need to consult the charter in which that independence had originally been asserted.

Soon after the official British recognition of American independence, European students of public law incorporated the Declaration into the modern positive law of nations. For example, the British politician and Board of Trade member Charles Jenkinson included it in his 1785 collection of treaties, and indeed used it to mark the most recent moment in a period of international affairs that had begun with the Spanish recognition of the independence of the United Provinces in 1649: "By the Treaties made at Paris in 1783, another Revolution was acknowledged and confirmed, viz. that of the United States of America." Jenkinson placed the document between a Spanish declaration of 1771 concerning the Falkland Islands and the Franco-American treaty of 1778, as an equivalent document within the positive law of nations.[63] Martens's *Summary of the Law of Nations . . . of the Modern Nations of Europe* (1789) listed it, along with the Articles of Confederation, which these European commentators also construed as an international agreement entered into by thirteen free and independent states.[64]

The first generation of lawyers in the new American republic observed that the United States had entered the interna-

tional system at an especially propitious time in the history of
the law of nations. For example, when James Kent produced
the earliest digest of American law in 1826, he began his *Commentaries* with a chapter on the law of nations. This first chapter
opened with the assertion that "when the United States ceased
to be a part of the British empire, and assumed the character of
an independent nation, they became subject to that system
of rules which reason, morality, and custom, had established
among the civilized nations of Europe, as their public law." He
acknowledged that opinions differed as to whether the law of
nations was "a mere system of positive institutions" or "essentially the same as the law of nature, applied to the conduct of
nations."[65]

Because the authors of the Declaration of Independence had
striven to make the document conform to the prevailing norms
of the late eighteenth-century international order, it had been
jurisprudentially eclectic. It was neither wholly naturalist nor
exclusively positivist. Its argument was partly grounded in natural law, but it concluded with a positive statement of "all the
. . . Acts and Things which Independent States may of right
do." By the third quarter of the eighteenth century the authority of natural law theory in Britain, France, and Germany was
beginning to wane after almost two centuries of ascendancy.[66]
It was therefore somewhat ironic that the language of individual
natural rights—which in its modern form had sprung from this

tradition—should have become so prominent during the era of the American and French Revolutions: only as the philosophical underpinnings that had made sense of it gave way did that language gain a temporary, though far from permanent, hegemony over political discourse. By the end of the eighteenth century, in Europe at least, the notion of natural rights was apparently "an idea whose time had come too late in politics to coincide with its philosophical respectability."[67]

The rights claims of the Declaration itself played little part in American political discourse in the first forty years of the Republic. Five of the first state constitutions—Maryland (1776), North Carolina (1776), Pennsylvania (1776), Georgia (1777), and South Carolina (1778)—referred to the fact that the colonies had been declared independent, but only the New York constitution (1777) quoted the Declaration at length in its preamble. Many of these state constitutions enumerated various rights to life, liberty, and property, or based a right to pursue happiness and freedom on the belief that all men were born equal and independent, but they did so in language mostly drawn from other documents, especially George Mason's draft of the Virginia Declaration of Rights.[68]

The first imitation of the Declaration within North America affirmed the primacy of the rights of states over the rights of individuals. Inspired by the example of the United States, the inhabitants of the New Hampshire Grants declared their independence from Great Britain and from the state of New York in January 1777 to form their own "separate, free and independent jurisdiction or state," at first called New Connecticut but from June 1777 better known as Vermont.[69] "The State of *Vermont* . . . has a natural right to independence," argued one of its defenders in 1780. "They have declared to the world that they are, and of right ought to be, a free independant State."[70]

The United States refused to recognize an independent Vermont because it presented such an obvious challenge to the territorial integrity of the states that had succeeded the boundaries and jurisdictions of the previously existing colonies. Others beyond New York and Congress shared this fear of further fragmentation. "If every district so disposed, may for themselves determine that they are not within the claim of the thirteen states . . . we may soon have ten hundred states, all free and independent," observed a New Hampshire Convention of towns in 1780.[71] This opposition to further claims to independence, and the insistence on the legal principle of *uti possidetis*—which "provides that states emerging from decolonization shall presumptively inherit the colonial administrative borders that they held at the time of independence"—foreshadowed the almost uniform insistence on the maintenance of territorial integrity after a declaration of independence in later world history.[72] Vermont, however, remained separate both from Britain and from the United States until 1791, when it became the first independent republic to join the American union.

The language of the Declaration of Independence did not appear in the Federal Constitution. Indeed, the Declaration itself was barely mentioned in the debates of the Constitutional Convention; it was alluded to only once in the *Federalist Papers;* and it was otherwise rarely appealed to in the extensive debate on the ratification of the Constitution. In light of these conspicuous absences from American public debate, it comes as little surprise that Alexis de Tocqueville did not mention the Declaration in *Democracy in America* (1835–1840).

In an age of bitter partisan strife between Federalists and Jeffersonian Republicans, the Declaration had come to seem like a dangerously francophile, anti-British document, and a charter for potential revolution against all established governments. Its claims to natural rights and to a right of revolution had sounded suspiciously like the "Jacobinical" tenets of the French Revolution. Its catalogue of grievances against King George III (who after all reigned until 1820) also rendered it distinctly anti-British even when Britain and the United States stood formally against the threats of the French Directory and, later, Napoleon. Only after the War of 1812 did the Declaration itself come to be celebrated with the same cross-party national fervor as the Fourth of July itself. It was in precisely this period that the Declaration became a national icon. The first engravings and reprintings of the document were produced for display in homes and official buildings in 1817. The following year, John Trumbull exhibited his painting of the signing, originally sketched in 1786, to large crowds in Boston. In 1823, John Quincy Adams commissioned William J. Stone, a British-born printer in Washington, D.C., to produce facsimiles on vellum of the engrossed parchment version of the Declaration. Two hundred lavish copies were distributed to the nation's state houses and colleges, as well as to the surviving signers and the marquis de Lafayette.[73]

It was in light of this renewed interest that the second paragraph of the Declaration began its progress toward becoming the heart of the Declaration's meaning in the United States. Once independence had become an uncontested fact, Americans had little need to remember the assertions of independent statehood in the Declaration's opening and closing paragraphs. When peace had been restored with Britain, and the precise incidents that lay behind the grievances in the main body of the Declaration had been forgotten, all of substance that remained to be revered was the second paragraph.

The Declaration's original motivation and its cosmopolitan appeal to the "Opinions of Mankind" were lost to a nationalistic veneration of the document as a whole. Selective attention was paid only to its abstract claims rather than to its import as a document with international implications.

The natural rights claims of the second paragraph "gradually eclipsed altogether the document's assertion of the right to revolution" only in the 1820s; before then, most American "citations of the Declaration were usually drawn from its final paragraph."[74] In 1831 Sándor Bölöni Farkas, a Hungarian aristocrat traveling in the United States, neatly captured the significance of the document for Americans when in his account of the widespread American cult of the Declaration he noted that it bore no traces of the monarchical grants and charters found in Europe. Instead, "its language is entirely that of natural law."[75] In this judgment he echoed John Quincy Adams, who in 1821 distinguished the Declaration from earlier historic agreements between nobles and their princes, such as the Magna Carta: "Here was no great charter of Runnimead, yielded and accepted as a grant of royal bounty."[76]

Beginning in the late 1820s, various groups across the United States imitated the Declaration as they pressed their own particular claims against a range of domestic—and occasionally foreign—tyrants and oppressors. It is a striking fact that it was three Britons, and not American-born citizens, who first used the Declaration in this way. The utopian socialist Robert Owen proposed in 1829 a "Declaration of Mental Independence" to free Americans from private property, organized religion, and marriage. On July 4, 1832, a Scotswoman and follower of Owen, Frances Wright, argued in Philadelphia that the American Revolution would be incomplete without guarantees of free education, free labor, and retirement benefits for all working people. In a similar spirit, the English-born journalist George Henry Evans produced "The Working Men's Declaration of Independence" in the same year.[77]

The Declaration almost literally became American scripture when a Baptist journal published a Declaration of Independence from the "Satanic Crown and Kingdom" in August 1836 that was reprinted in the Cape Colony less than six months later.[78] As if to counter the cosmopolitan currents of circulation that these declarations represented, members of the white anti-Catholic, anti-immigrant Native American Convention issued a Declaration of Principles patterned after the Declaration in Philadelphia on July 4, 1845, "for the purpose of awakening their countrymen to a sense of the evils already experienced from foreign intrusion and usurpation."[79] Two weeks later, on July 19, 1845, the Women's Rights Convention, meeting in Seneca Falls, New York, issued the most enduring of all these early nineteenth-century imitations of the Declaration, Elizabeth Cady Stanton's Declaration of Sentiments, which held that "all men and women are created equal" and submitted to a candid world the "history of the repeated injuries and usurpations on the part of man toward women."[80]

By means of these imitations, and as a result of its sanctification among other monuments of the founding era, the Declaration became domesticated and Americanized for specifically national purposes. Gradually, only supporters of slavery and Southern secession came to insist that the Declaration's central message had been its announcement of independence. They did so not least to sap the increasing cultural prestige of the Declaration's enumeration of rights, resistance, and equality, lest they should be claimed by those to whom they had so obviously been denied: the enslaved.[81] As the proslavery propagandist George Fitzhugh put it in *Cannibals All!* (1857), the American Revolution "had nothing more to do with philosophy than the weaning of a calf. It was the act of a people seeking national independence, not the Utopian scheme of speculative philosophers, seeking to establish human equality and social perfection."[82] "All the bombastic absurdity in our Declaration of Independence about the inalienable rights of man," he later argued during the Civil War, "had about as much to do with the occasion as would a sermon or oration on the teething of a child or the kittening of a cat."[83]

Abraham Lincoln sought to combat such sentiments by his repeated invocations and exegeses of the Declaration before and during the American Civil War. He did so by recalling that the Declaration had in fact held two messages, one in 1776 and one for the future. Lincoln argued that to reduce the Declaration to its contingent purpose in 1776 was to render it a dead letter, of no present relevance. If it were simply a declaration of national independence, then its work had been done decades earlier: "Why that object having been effected some eighty years ago, the Declaration is of no practical use now—mere rubbish—old wadding left to rot on the battle-field after the victory is won." On the contrary, Lincoln stressed that there was a universal and enduring message in the Declaration that could be found in its second paragraph. "All honor to Jefferson," he later wrote in 1859, "to the man who, in the concrete pressure of a struggle for national independence by a single people, had the coolness, forecast, and capacity to introduce into a merely revolutionary document, an abstract truth, applicable to all men and all times."[84]

The application of that "abstract truth" as a yardstick to measure the antebellum United States was hardly likely to be reassuring. The free black abolitionist David Walker had made this point twenty years before Lincoln wrote. Walker concluded his *Appeal to the Colored Citizens of the World* (1829) with a call to white Americans to "compare your own language . . . extracted from your Declaration of Independence, with your cruelties and murders inflicted by your cruel and unmerciful fathers and yourselves on our fathers and on us."[85] The same point would be summoned with greatest force by the former slave Frederick Douglass before an audience in Rochester, New York, on July 5, 1852. In his towering oration, "What to the Slave is the Fourth of July?" Douglass told his mostly white audience that that hallowed day was "the birthday of your National Independence, and of your political freedom" and that "the Declaration of Independence is the RING-BOLT to the chain of your nation's destiny." He reminded those present of Richard Henry Lee's resolution of July 2, 1776, but failed to elaborate further on the grievances that had led to independence. Instead, he dramatically turned the tables on his listeners, arguing that this holiday was theirs and theirs alone: "I am not included within the pale of this glorious anniversary! Your high independence only reveals the immeasurable distance between us. . . . This Fourth [of] July is *yours,* not *mine. You* may rejoice, *I* must mourn." The ineradicable national stains of slavery and the internal slave trade, the weakness of the abolitionist movement, and the connivance of the churches at the perpetuation of human bondage all confirmed that "there is not a nation on earth guilty of practices, more shocking and bloody, than are the people of these United States, at this very hour."[86]

Douglass hammered home his assault on his audience's consciences by setting the "national inconsistencies" of the United States in both international and ultimately global contexts. White Americans, he charged, readily condemned tyranny in Russia or Austria but not in Virginia or Carolina. They "shed tears over fallen Hungary" but wept not for the wronged American slave. They burned for the liberty of France or Ireland "but are as cold as an iceberg at the thought of liberty for the enslaved of America." Such was their attachment to the Declaration that Americans asserted "before the world, and are understood by the world to declare," that they held it self-evident that all men were created equal and endowed by their Creator with certain rights, among them life, liberty, and the pursuit of happiness, "and yet, you hold securely, in . . . bondage . . . *a seventh part* of the inhabitants of your country."[87]

Perhaps when the world had felt larger, communications had been slower, and nations had been more self-sufficient, a people could escape accountability for such spectacular hypocrisy, Douglass argued. After 1776, and in light of the contraction of the globe, they could no longer hide so easily from the judging eyes of humanity:

> While drawing encouragement from the Declaration of Independence, the great principles it contains, and the genius of American Institutions, my spirit is also cheered by the obvious tendencies of the age. Nations do not now stand in the same relation to each other that they did ages ago. No nation can now shut itself up from the surrounding world, and trot round in the same old path of its fathers without interference. . . . Walled cities and empires have become unfashionable. The arm of commerce has

borne away the gates of the strong city. Intelligence is pen-
etrating the darkest corners of the globe. It makes its path-
way over and under the sea, as well as on the earth. Wind,
steam, and lightning are its chartered agents. Oceans no
longer divide, but link nations together. From Boston to
London is now a holiday excursion. Space is comparatively
annihilated.[88]

With this precocious appreciation of what we would now call
globalization, Douglass heralded a new moment in the international histories of the United States and the Declaration of
Independence.[89] Seventy-six years on from 1776, the United
States was still not completely free soil, yet at least it had a
moral imperative to live up to, derived from the claims of its
founding document.

The Declaration was now known to the whole world, and
that world would judge America according to the document's
standards. Commerce and communications bound peoples together as never before; one result of this interconnectedness
would be a greater sharing of political and religious languages
around the globe.[90] Douglass was surely correct to link the "en-
couragement" that could be derived from the Declaration with
the more far-reaching "tendencies of the age" to dissolve cultural particularisms and to bring distinct peoples into closer

contact with one another. Yet he would soon prove to be mistaken about one defining feature of the age. "Walled cities" may have begun to fall around the globe by the mid-nineteenth century, but empires were far from going out of fashion: quite the contrary, in fact. Among the world leaders who sent congratulations to the United States on the centennial of independence in 1876 were the Russian emperor, Alexander II, the German emperor, William I, the emperor of Austria, Franz Joseph II, and the emperor of Brazil, Dom Pedro II.[91] That same year, the British Royal Titles Act made Queen Victoria empress of India. A century after 1776, empires were certainly not in retreat; they were on the march and gaining ground across the world.

The Declaration of Independence had introduced the United States into an exclusive world of states in 1776. At the same moment, it had also led America into a world inhabited by empires, both the great territorial units of Eurasia and the European maritime empires that projected their power across oceans to span the whole globe. During the first half of the nineteenth century, the United States would be joined by a host of new republics in the Americas and by other emerging states in Europe. The world of empires, however, would not pass until the second half of the twentieth century. By the American bicentennial in 1976, it had almost entirely disappeared, though remnants of it linger with us still. Its gradual but accelerating dissolution would be marked by a series of declarations of independence generically similar to—and sometimes modeled on—a document that Americans came to revere as their own, but which had become over time the possession of the whole world.

CHAPTER THREE

A World of Declarations

The American Revolution was the first outbreak of a contagion of sovereignty that has swept the world in the centuries since 1776. Its influence spread first to the Low Countries and then to the Caribbean, Spanish America, the Balkans, West Africa, and Central Europe in the decades up to 1848. The infection then lay dormant until after the First World War, when it appeared again in Central Europe and East Asia. The next pandemic sprang up in Asia and Africa after the Second World War. Other outbreaks in the Baltics, the Balkans, and Eastern Europe after 1989 culminated in the dissolution of the Soviet Union, Yugoslavia, and Czechoslovakia in 1990–1993.

Declarations of independence were among the primary symptoms of this contagion of sovereignty. They were diagnoses, too, in that they often defined the nature of the epidemic in the language of state sovereignty. As documents that announced the emergence of new states—or, in some cases, the re-emergence of older polities— they marked the transition from subordination within an empire to independence alongside other states.[1]

Since 1776, more than one hundred such documents have been issued on behalf of regional or nationalist groups; many more local declarations have also appeared in places such as Central America in the 1820s, in China after the Revolution of 1911, and in Korea in 1918–1919, to mark the aspirations of substate entities.[2] Some of these declarations stated a desire for independence yet to come; most marked a *fait accompli*. Many, like the American Declaration itself, listed grievances to justify the independence that they claimed; relatively few, however, contained a declaration of individual rights that paralleled the second paragraph of the American Declaration. In this way, they confirmed the main message of that document to the world: that it was an assertion of the rights of states among other states rather than an enumeration of the rights of individuals against their governors.

Taken together, the declarations of independence issued around the globe since the late eighteenth century mark a major transition in world history: in this era a world of states emerged from a world of empires. States now have jurisdiction

over every part of the Earth's land surface, with the major exception of Antarctica. The only states of exception—such as
Guantánamo Bay—are the exceptions created by states.[3] At
least potentially, states also have jurisdiction over every inhabit-
ant of the planet: to be a stateless person is to wander an inhos-
pitable world in quest of a state's protection. The blanketing of
the Earth with states is one of the most overlooked effects of
globalization. Many of its critics have held globalization to be
the greatest solvent of state sovereignty. However, globalization
has also been one of the state's greatest propellants around the
world. Over the past two centuries and more, the state has
merged with indigenous forms of political organization and
emotional identification to create the system of states that now
covers all the inhabited world.

The creation of a world of states has been largely the work
of the last two centuries, especially the last fifty years.[4] It has
combined two broad developments: the consolidation of states
out of lesser polities or territories and the dissolution of empires into states. The result has been a striking pattern of contraction and then expansion in the number of polities since the
late Middle Ages. In some regions we can discern a long-term
pattern of cultural integration and political centralization. In
Southeast Asia, for example, "between 1340 and 1820 some 23
independent . . . kingdoms collapsed into three."[5] A similar
pattern is obvious in Europe, where discrete political units de-

creased from roughly 1,000 in the fourteenth century to fewer than 500 by the early sixteenth century, to roughly 350 on the eve of the French Revolution, including the pocket-handker-chief principalities of the Holy Roman Empire.[6]

By 1900 Europe had only 25 nation-states at the most gener-ous count. In 1945, 50 states from every part of the world gathered at the San Francisco Conference to found the United Nations, though some—India, the Philippines, Byelorussia, and Ukraine, for example—were still formally parts of an empire or multinational confederation.[7] Between 1950 and 1993, more than 100 new states were created by secession, decolonization, or dissolution. As of July 4, 2006, 192 states divide the bulk of the Earth's surface and its populations among themselves. They are represented at a world body rather inaptly named the United Nations (UN):[8] "inaptly," not because the UN is obvi-ously far from united, but rather because its members are for-mally states and not nations, of which there are potentially many hundreds, even thousands, across the globe.[9] Strictly, the United Nations should have been called "the United *States*," but that name had already been taken by the representatives of an-other, rather different, group of political actors in July 1776.

States made empires, and empires dissolved into states. Em-pires are structures of political and economic interference that organize their component parts hierarchically.[10] They thus rep-resent the major conditions that statehood is designed to escape.[11] Statehood implies the absence of external interference in internal affairs as well as formal equality in relations with other states. Inviolability and equality are at the heart of this conception of external sovereignty. Only if all states mutually respect those requirements can any state be secure in its own independence. For this basic reason, "sovereignty is contagious: once any community becomes a state, neighboring communities respond in kind."[12]

Since 1776, there have been four historically distinct moments of declaring independence, all of which have coincided with the break up of empires: in the first half of the nineteenth century, in the immediate aftermaths of the First and Second World Wars, and in the years 1990–1993. The first, between 1790 and 1848, coincided with the so-called Age of Revolutions— American, French, Haitian, and European—and encompassed the New World of the Americas as well as the Old World of Europe. This period comprised what might be called the first Eurasian rights moment, when conceptions of rights, both collective and individual, first animated movements for independence, autonomy, and liberation across the world. In the wake of the American Revolution, wrote the marquis de Condorcet, "the rights of men were nobly upheld and expounded without restriction or reserve, in writings that circulated freely from the shores of the Neva to those of the Guadalquivir."[13] By the early nineteenth century, such writings had spread from the Appalachians to the Balkans, Bengal, and beyond.

The documents of the American Revolution contributed less to the making of this Eurasian rights moment than did the French Revolutionary rights documents and the traditions of British liberalism. For example, the late eighteenth-century Greek republican patriot Rhigas Velestinlis called for uprisings against Ottoman despotism in a French Revolutionary language that spoke of a sovereign people and their individual rights. Not long before he became the first martyr of the Greek independence movement in 1798, Rhigas wrote a revolutionary proclamation, a declaration of rights, and a constitution for a future Hellenic Republic.[14] These documents foreshadowed the rights claims of the declaration of independence issued by the Hellenic National Assembly in January 1822.[15] Around the same time, the Bengali reformer Rammohan Roy, inspired in part by the American and French Revolutions, attacked the despotism of the East India Company and defended the historic rights of Indians.[16]

The first wave of declarations of independence outside the United States—in Haiti, Spanish America, Greece, Hungary, and Liberia, for example—retained an identifiably American component. As Condorcet had put it in 1786, "it is not enough that the rights of man be written in the books of philosophers and the hearts of virtuous men; the ignorant and weak man

must be able to read them in the example of a great people. America has given us this example. The act that declared
American independence is a simple and sublime statement of
these sacred and long-forgotten rights."[17] Perhaps because the
American Revolution was still a vivid memory in this era, the
declarations of independence issued during this phase showed
more of a debt to the American example than would those in
the later moments, for example, during the twentieth century.

The second significant moment of declaring independence
came after the First World War, with the collapse of the great
land empires of the Ottomans, the Romanovs, and the Habsburgs, as well as the outpouring of demands for self-determination from the Balkans to Korea.[18] During this moment, individualistic accounts of rights gave way to movements for the rights
of nations and peoples. "No right anywhere exists to hand peoples about from sovereignty to sovereignty as if they were
property," Woodrow Wilson told the United States Senate in
January 1917.[19] At least, that might have been true for parts of
Europe in the aftermath of the First World War, but it would
not remain so for the colonized world beyond Europe and the
Americas.

The high tide of nineteenth-century European nationalism
coincided with the expansion and proliferation of European
empires, within Eurasia and around the globe. With imperialism came a hierarchical racialism that set its face firmly against

claims of human equality and universal rights to life, liberty, and the pursuit of happiness. The British foreign secretary Arthur Balfour spoke for this tendency during the debate on the racial equality clause at the Versailles Conference in 1919: "the proposition taken from the Declaration of Independence, that all men are created equal . . . was an eighteenth century proposition which he did not believe was true. He believed it was true in a certain sense that all men of a particular nation were created equal, but not that a man in Central Africa was created equal to a European."[20] Such suspicion of individualistic assertions of rights helped to ensure that declarations of independence from this moment would generally steer clear of such claims except when they were specifically appealing for American support, as in the case of the Czechoslovak declaration of independence of 1918.[21]

The third great moment of declaring independence lasted from the end of the Second World War until the zenith of decolonization in 1975. The Atlantic Charter of 1941 (which had been explicitly framed to exclude anti-imperial assertions of self-determination),[22] the Universal Declaration of Human Rights (1948), the European Convention on Human Rights (1950), and such later documents as the United Nations Declaration on the Granting of Independence to Colonial Countries and Peoples (1960) made this the first—and still ongoing— truly global rights moment in world history.[23] During this period, some seventy new states were created from the wreckage of the British, French, and Portuguese overseas empires, mostly in Africa and Asia. Declarations of independence joined other instruments of independence devised for extinguishing empires.

Most of the declarations from this third moment marked the end, not the beginning, of the liberation struggles from which they sprang. With a greater array of precedents from which to choose, leaders of independence movements rarely alluded directly to the American Declaration, but instead often drew inspiration from contemporary anticolonial struggles. To take just one example from this period: the timing of the East Timorese declaration of independence from Portuguese colonial rule of November 28, 1975, was directly inspired by the MPLA (Movimento Popular de Liberação de Angola) declaration of independence from Portugal (November 11, 1975), which had been issued in Luanda, Angola, earlier that same month.[24] The circuits within which declarations traveled no longer originated only from Europe and the neo-European settlements of the Americas but transmitted political models around other, extra-European overseas empires even as they collapsed and fragmented.

The fourth and most recent moment for declaring independence was also the most concentrated in world history. Between 1990 and 1993, more than thirty states became indepen-

dent or regained independence. All but one—Eritrea—emerged
from the collapse of the Soviet Union, the break up of the Yu-
goslav Federation, or the consensual dissolution of Czechoslovakia into the Czech and Slovak Republics.[25] With an average of
ten declarations of independence a year, this era was even more
explosive than that of the 1810s and 1820s, when Spanish
America had fragmented under the long-distance impact of Napoleon's assault on the Iberian Peninsula. It seems unlikely that
there will ever again be a profusion of declarations of independence comparable to these early nineteenth- and late twentieth-century explosions.

As I write this book, a handful of declarations still await recognition: for example, those for Kosovo (1991) and Somaliland
(1991), each of which betokens different forms of unfinished
business pertaining to federal dissolution in the Balkans and decolonization in the Horn of Africa.[26] Similarly, the very possibility of a declaration of Taiwanese independence would create
an intractable conflict out of an apparently insoluble dilemma,
so firmly has mainland China set its face against the secession of
what it maintains is still a province of the People's Republic.
For the moment, though, the contagion of sovereignty seems to
have entered a period of general remission.

The American Declaration of Independence had been the first
in history to identify external sovereignty ("all . . . Acts and
Things which INDEPENDENT STATES may of right do") with

independence: that equation would prove to be as lastingly in-
fluential as the very form of the Declaration itself. The American Revolution was also the first secessionist revolt to succeed after Vattel's conception of independence became the
touchstone of external sovereignty. The ultimate success of the
Americans' claim to independence encouraged others to follow
their example, not only in claiming statehood as an escape from
empire, but also in declaring independence as the mark of sovereignty. The earliest imitations of the Declaration in Europe
and beyond set the pattern for most later documents by taking
the Declaration's opening and closing sentences as their template while overlooking the self-evident truths of the second
paragraph.

The first imitation of the Declaration of 1776 outside North
America drew its inspiration in just this way from the Declaration's opening and closing paragraphs. The *Manifesto of the Province of Flanders,* issued by the Flemish Estates in 1790, detailed
grievances against the Austrian monarchy of Emperor Joseph II.
The bulk of the Flemish manifesto dealt with historical claims
to traditional rights, much like those that had constituted the
body of the Dutch Act of Abjuration two centuries earlier. Its
authors argued that the assault by the House of Austria on those
rights, and the emperor's failure to heed the petitions of his
subjects, had returned the Flemish people to a state of nature in
possession of their natural rights of liberty and independence.[27]

That same year, a French-language history of the Ameri-

can Revolution, accompanied by translations of the state constitutions and the Declaration of Independence, appeared in
Ghent.[28] The French version of the Declaration returned the
assertions of the closing paragraph to the language of Vattel
that had helped to inspire the Declaration itself.[29] It was from
this version that the Flemish rebels drew their final declaration:
"before the Supreme Judge of the World who knows the justice
of our cause, we solemnly publish and declare in the name of
the People that this Province is and of right ought to be a Free
and Independent State; that it has been absolved from all allegiance to the Emperor Joseph II."[30] The Flemish *Manifesto* thus
combined the structure of an earlier genre of political protest
with the American Declaration's distinctive assertion of statehood as independence. A similarly syncretic appreciation of the
Declaration became possible in 1798, when it appeared alongside the French Declaration of the Rights of Man and the Citizen and the Constitution of 1795, as well as the 1797 Constitutions of the Cisalpine Republic created by the French in
Lombardy and the Romagna, and of the Ligurian Republic they
created in Genoa. As if to offer the Declaration to the widest
European audience, the text appeared in four parallel columns,
in English, German, French, and Italian.[31]

The American Declaration also provided the primary model
for the first great wave of declarations of independence that
swept the trans-Atlantic world in the first half of the nineteenth

century. The first such declaration in the Americas after 1776, the Haitian declaration of January 1, 1804, was also the exception to prove this rule. The Haitian document set the seal on the most successful slave revolt in the western hemisphere by announcing the existence of the first independent black republic. The first draft of the declaration had been written by "an admirer of the work of Jefferson" who modeled it on the American Declaration. Some, however, felt it was too passionless to serve its inspirational purpose. "To draw up the act of independence," wrote Louis Boisrond-Tonnerre, the free black author of the revised Haitian declaration, "we need the skin of a white man for parchment, his skull for an inkwell, his blood for ink, and a bayonet for a pen!"[32]

Over the night of December 31, 1803, Boisrond-Tonnerre himself wrote a new declaration addressed to the people of Haiti in which he proclaimed that "it is necessary to live independent, or die. Independence or Death!" In stark contrast to the American Declaration, which had spoken of "British brethren" even in the act of breaking loose from them, the Haitian declaration proclaimed that the inhabitants of Haiti had no kinship with the French, who had deprived them of their liberty for so long: "What have we in common with that bloody-minded people?" The Haitian people had dared to free themselves from their bondage and to make their island free soil: better, then, to die protecting that freedom than to live as slaves again: "Swear then to live free and independent, and to prefer death to every thing that would lead to replace you under the yoke."[33]

The Haitian declaration of independence was directed to a domestic audience rather than to the candid world and was proclaimed to a crowd in Gonaïves, north of Port-au-Prince, on the morning of January 1, 1804. With French, Spanish, and British military forces ranged against them, the Haitians had no obvious source of support among the powers of the earth; nor with this declaration did they claim to be joining that select group. Instead, they were asserting firmly and clearly the end of slavery and thereby threatening the stability of remaining slave powers like the United States. They affirmed the end of all connection with France, whether political or sentimental, and asserted also their triumph over slavery. Freedom and independence were more than mere metaphors or abstract norms of international law in this context: they were animating ideals and hard-won prizes.

The Haitian example would soon show that the common possession of declarations of independence was no guarantee of kinship between new states. The first republic in the Americas—the United States—did not hasten to recognize the second, Haiti. Under the presidency of the American Declaration's prime author, Thomas Jefferson, the United States refused formally to acknowledge Haiti for fear that recognition would only incite further slave revolts on the mainland.[34] Not until 1862 would Abraham Lincoln extend American recognition to Haiti, almost four decades after France itself had recognized Haitian independence in 1825.[35] This American reluctance to acknowledge an independent Haiti foreshadowed later occasions, such as the declaration of independence of the Philippines in 1898, when domestic interests would override the desire of the United States to reproduce and multiply independent sovereignties in its own hemisphere and beyond.[36]

The United States was ultimately more encouraging to the spread of sovereignty in Central and South America in the early decades of the nineteenth century, despite its attempts to remain aloof from the entanglements of foreign affairs.[37] Jefferson himself had begun fomenting resistance to the Iberian empires as early as 1786, when he met clandestinely in Nîmes with José Joaquim Maia e Barbalho, a Brazilian medical student who went by the pseudonym "Vendek." Vendek would later carry the American Declaration to Brazil.[38] The Declaration does not seem to have been translated into Portuguese until 1821, a year after the Portuguese metropole had effectively declared their independence from Brazil.[39] When independence came to Brazil itself in 1822, it was declared orally, by the transplanted Portuguese prince Dom Pedro I, and showed no evidence of having been influenced by the American Declaration.[40]

Spanish-American authorities had attempted to prevent the spread of anti-imperial propaganda by banning the circulation of the Declaration and other documents of the American Revolution.[41] However, the Declaration was still widely transmitted and translated in South and Central America. In 1802–1803, the New Englanders Richard Cleveland and William Shaler distributed translations of the Declaration and the United States Constitution among both creoles in Chile and Indians in Mexico, "for the better promotion of the embryo cause" of their liberation. In 1811, the Colombian Miguel de Pombo prefaced a translation of the U.S. Constitution with a version of the Declaration. That same year, the Venezuelan exile Manuel García de Sena translated the Declaration and the Constitution alongside extracts from Paine's *Common Sense* and other works. A decade later, after the restoration in 1820 of the Spanish Constitution of 1812, the Ecuadorian exile in Philadelphia Vicente Rocafuerte also translated Paine alongside the major American political documents—including the Declaration, which he called "the true political decalogue"—for the benefit of his countrymen and other Spanish-Americans.[42]

The first great waves of declarations of independence, which came from Spanish America in the 1810s and 1820s, were indebted to the American Declaration, as these zealous promoters of the American example had hoped.[43] The years between the French invasion of the Peninsula in 1808 and the restoration of the monarchy in 1814 witnessed a series of movements for autonomy among the Spanish kingdoms of the New World. With the collapse of the Bourbon monarchy in Spain, Spanish Americans argued that sovereignty returned to the various American kingdoms. They were able to elect representatives to the Spanish Cortes from 1810 to 1814 and were included in the nation whose sovereignty was enshrined in the 1812 Constitution of Cadiz, which was annulled with the return of King Ferdinand VII to the Spanish throne. During these years, the majority of their "leaders demanded *equality* rather than *independence:* They sought *home rule* not *separation* from the Spanish Crown."[44]

The major exception to the Spanish-American desire for autonomy rather than independence during these early years was Venezuela, geographically the closest of all the Spanish captaincies-general to the Caribbean and Europe, and hence the one most immediately affected by political developments along Atlantic routes of communication. When a General Congress of Venezuela met in March 1811, its members swore to uphold the rights of the *patria* and King Ferdinand. Within weeks, however, public pressure and maneuvering by radical deputies brought the Congress to discuss an *acta de independencia* on July 5, 1811. Congress ratified the act two days later and published it on Bastille Day, 1811, with the accompaniment of a French-inspired tricolor.[45]

The Venezuelan declaration of independence owed much more to the American example than to any French model. It presented "the authentic and well-known facts" of the disorders that had afflicted the Spanish monarchy since 1808 to argue that because Spain had denied Venezuela proper representation, declared war against it, and subjected it to other indignities, the Spanish authorities had broken the contractual basis of their relationship. Venezuela's freedom and independence "to take amongst the powers of the earth the place of equality which the Supreme Being and Nature assign to us" could now be recovered. The representatives "declare[d] solemnly to the world, that [Venezuela's] united Provinces are, and ought to be, from this day, by act and right, Free, Sovereign, and Independent States" with the power "to do and transact every act, in like manner as other free and independent States."[46]

Similar words and sentiments could be found in the *acta de independencia* issued by the *junta* of Cartagena, which broke away formally from the Spanish Monarchy, and effectively from the United Provinces of New Granada, in November 1811.[47] Later Latin American declarations would retain the assertion of sovereignty without any extensive cataloguing of grievances—a justification often left to manifestoes that accompanied or succeeded the *actas de independencia*—or abstract justifications for rebellion or separation. In this way, the United Provinces of the Rio de la Plata (Argentina) proclaimed in July 1816 that they were "a nation free and independent of Ferdinand VII" in language drawn from the American Declaration that affirmed the rectitude of their intentions and pledged themselves to the protection of their lives, properties, and honor.[48] Eighteen months later, in January 1 8 1 8, the terse independence proclamation of Chile similarly stated that "the Continental Territory of Chile, and its adjacent Islands, form in fact and right, a free, independent and sovereign State."[49] By adopting the language of the American Declaration, and by elaborating cadenzas on its structure, these Spanish-American documents established declarations of independence as a genre originating in the American example.

The profusion of *actas de independencia* issued by Spanish America's municipal councils, regional *juntas*, cities, provinces, and kingdoms during the late 1 8 1 0s and 1 8 2 0s mostly drew on Spanish understandings of sovereignty as residing in the autonomy of specific *pueblos* rather than in particular nations or states.[50] This was especially evident in Central America, where, as the first historian of the region's independence movements lamented in 1 8 3 2, "the hotheads [of Guatemala] founded the anarchic dogma that the pueblos, on becoming independent from Spain, recovered their natural liberty and were free to form new societies as it suited them in the new order of things."[51] Yet it was not always clear just how free and independent these *pueblos* were in making their decisions for independence: the apparently overwhelming support in Lima for a Peruvian declaration of independence (July 15, 1821), which more than 3,500 people signed, has been persuasively attributed to force, fear, and self-interest rather than to any fervor for self-government outside the Spanish monarchy.[52]

The American Declaration provided the generic model for other declarations of independence in North America, Africa, and Eastern Europe in the 1830s and 1840s, with the break up of the Mexican Empire and the springtime of revolutions in Eastern Europe. For example, the Texas declaration of independence (March 2, 1836) affirmed the necessity of "severing our political connection with the Mexican people, and assuming an independent attitude among the peoples of the earth" as "a free, sovereign, and independent republic."[53] This declaration would be almost unique before the twentieth century in marking the successful cession of one people from another that had already declared its independence, as Mexico had done in a series of documents culminating in the "Act of Independence of the [Mexican] Empire" (September 28, 1821).[54] A further declaration of independence from Mexico issued in Alta California on November 7, 1836, demanded that the territory be considered "a free and sovereign state," but, unlike Texas, California did not immediately succeed in establishing its sovereignty outside the Mexican Empire.[55]

Alone among declarations of independence before the twentieth century, the Liberian declaration of independence (July
26, 1847) enshrined a recognition of "certain inalienable rights;
among these are life, liberty, and the right to acquire, possess,
enjoy, and defend property." This, the first declaration of independence in Africa, was composed by the Virginia-born Afri-
can-American journalist and politician Hilary Teague, and began with a declaration that the Republic of Liberia was "a free,
sovereign, and independent state."[56]

Commentators have often denied that the Liberian declaration owed anything to the American Declaration, on the
grounds that it proposed no right of rebellion and merely affirmed the existing sovereignty of Liberia.[57] However, the Liberian document did parallel the structure of the American Declaration by listing the grievances that drove the first settlers
of Liberia out of the United States. It then explained how
the American Colonization Society—the colony's first promoters—had gradually withdrawn their oversight to leave the people of Liberia to govern themselves. It addressed itself to "the
candid consideration of the civilized world." Finally, in keeping
with the mid-nineteenth-century norms of international law,
the Liberians used their document to "appeal to the nations of
Christendom . . . to extend to us, that comity which marks
the friendly intercourse of civilized and independent communi-

ties."[58] Circumstances, and prevailing norms, may have changed since 1776, but the Liberian declaration's debts to its American original were unmistakable.

Similarly for this period, Lajos Kossuth's Hungarian declaration of independence (April 14, 1849), "a document written by Hungarian lawyer-politicians for Hungarian lawyer-politicians," affirmed Hungary's "inalienable natural rights . . . to occupy the position of an independent European state" and the fact that along with Transylvania it "constitute[d] a free, independent sovereign state." This document may be the longest declaration of independence ever issued. Much of it narrated three centuries of Hungarian history as a sequence of oppressions by the Habsburg monarchy, with neither an explicit enumeration of rights nor a statement of abstract principles for rebellion. However, it did openly appeal to other European states for recognition, and, no doubt with this aim in mind, the Hungarian government had the document translated and widely disseminated.[59] Kossuth, the declaration's prime author, had long been—and would long remain—a great admirer of the United States and its Revolution.[60] His announcement of independence repaid that admiration with a document of flattering imitation, albeit one that lacked the concision and flexibility of the American original.

As if to confirm the equation of independence with sovereignty, it was also in this moment that the leaders of the united

Maori tribes of the North Island of New Zealand signed a "Declaration of the Independence of New Zealand" on October 28, 1835.[61] This document recognized the territorial sovereignty and landownership of the Maori only in order to allow British penetration of the islands before the French could lay claim to them. As the British Resident in New Zealand, James Busby, disingenuously explained the maneuver, "I have declared the Independence of New Zealand:—*that is,* my own Independence as Sovereign Chief," because "the establishment of the Independence of New Zealand, under the protection of the British Government, would be the most effectual mode of making the country a dependency of the British Empire, in every thing but the name."[62] But within a decade of the New Zealand declaration, the Maori insurgent against empire Hone Heke, whose land had been sold to Busby in 1835, attacked a British flagstaff, the symbol of imperial sovereignty, just after July 4, 1844. Heke was alleged to know both English and American history and may have been partly inspired by American independence almost seventy years earlier.[63] The American example could clearly cut both ways.

That example circulated throughout the white settler colonies of the remaining parts of the British Empire during the nineteenth century, where it helped to inspire rebellion in Canada in the late 1830s and in the Australian state of Victoria in the 1850s, as well as a precocious call for Australian independence in 1887. For example, during the 1837 revolts in Upper Canada, the Scottish journalist and politician William Lyon Mackenzie reprinted the Declaration in his Toronto newspaper, *The Constitution,* and helped to draft a "Declaration of the Reformers of the City of Toronto" that contrasted the advantages enjoyed by the post-Revolutionary United States with the plight of the Loyalists who had fled north across the new border and indicted the British king, William IV, with a list of grievances modeled on the Declaration's list of charges before paraphrasing its penultimate paragraphs ("Nor have we been wanting in attention to our British brethren. . . . They too have been deaf to justice and consanguinity.")[64]

The Declaration seems to have taken rather longer to be sympathetically received in Australia. For example, when the Sydney barrister and critic of Aboriginal rights Richard Windeyer alluded in an 1844 lecture to the individual rights laid out in "that noble declaration which proclaimed American Independence," he did so to pronounce them so self-evident that discussion of them "must ever be uncalled for in a community so purely British as to have no thought even of the possibility of here witholding the practical enjoyment of those rights from their brethren of any race or colour."[65] Disaffected miners on the goldfields of Victoria a decade later were not so complacent about their rights. A group of them constructed the Eureka Stockade in Ballarat in December 1854 to defend themselves against troops sent to quell their rioting at the imposition of license fees for digging, among other grievances. They raised a new blue-and-white flag over the stockade, emblazoned with the Southern Cross, and, according to some reports, one of their number read out a "Declaration of Independence" on December 1, 1854. No copy of this declaration survived. Nonetheless, when Karl Marx read a news report of the siege at the Eureka Stockade, he perceived an analogy with the American document. The gold-diggers were agitating "to obtain control over taxes and legislation," he wrote. "Here we see, in essence, motives similar to those which led to the Declaration of Independence of the United States, except that in Australia the conflict is initiated by the workers against the monopolists linked with the colonial bureaucracy."[66]

Australia would never issue a formal declaration of independence from Great Britain. The feminist and republican journalist Louisa Lawson, reflecting dimly on the monarchist celebrations of Queen Victoria's silver jubilee in 1887, did call for such a declaration of Australian independence in an editorial published on July 4 that year: "If this species of mania is to prevail in our colony, it is high time that the sensible and self respecting lifted up their voices for separation and independence."[67] When the founding fathers of the Australian Federation first met in 1891, they made no appeals to the American Declaration, though they had the American Constitution very

much before them as a possible model for an Australian constitution.[68] Australian grievances over continuing dependence on
Britain after Federation in 1901, and the great admiration of
many of Australia's early statesmen for the United States, could
conceivably have led to a declaration of independence, but they
did not.[69] Australia, like Canada, would ultimately gain legislative independence from Great Britain by the Statute of Westminster in 1931. It was thus the imperial Parliament that declared the independence of the Dominions in this sense, but it
would not stand for any further secessionist challenges, such as
the attempt by Western Australia to secede from the Australian
Federation in 1934–1935.[70]

More revealing of the influence of the Declaration in the second half of the nineteenth century are the declarations of independence by the states of the southern Confederacy. These
took quite literally the claims to sovereign statehood made in
the Declaration of 1776. For example, the "South Carolina
Declaration of Secession" (December 20, 1860) appropriated
both the language and the structure of the Declaration to justify
the state's much terser secession Ordinance. It recalled the history of the American troubles from 1765 to 1776 to argue that
thirteen separate states had agreed to the Declaration and then
had entered into the Articles of Confederation in 1778, all the
while maintaining their independent sovereignty, which was
then confirmed by the Peace of Paris in 1783: "each Colony be-

came and was recognized by the mother Country as a FREE, SOVEREIGN AND INDEPENDENT STATE." The document went on to argue that these states entered into the Constitution still subject to two principles derived from the Declaration itself: the right of self-government and the right to abolish any government that became destructive of the ends for which it was established. On these grounds, by using the logic of the Declaration to assert secession against union, the drafters asserted that "South Carolina has *resumed* her position among the nations of the world, as a separate and independent State; with full power to levy war, conclude peace, contract alliances, establish commerce, and to do all the other acts and things which independent States may of right do."[71] The following year Tennessee issued a "Declaration of Independence and Ordinance of Secession" (May 6, 1861), while the last state to secede, Kentucky, also declared itself to be a "free and independent state" on November 20, 1861.[72] The Unionist response to these claims was simply that they amounted to treason against the United States, the only government legitimately empowered to exercise independent sovereignty since 1787.[73]

The equation of independence with statehood, rather than with nationhood, became increasingly clear during the second half of the nineteenth century and helps to explain the otherwise paradoxical fact that there were almost no declarations of independence between 1849 and 1918, the period usually associated with the high tide of European nationalism. To be sure, various states did gain their independence during this period, among them those that emerged from the gradual dismemberment of the Ottoman Empire—for example, Romania, Serbia, Montenegro (all recognized as independent by the 1878 Treaty of Berlin), Bulgaria (1908), and Albania (1913)—and Norway, which dissolved its regal union with Sweden in 1905. However, they generally did so not by means of declarations of independence but by means of treaty, mutual divorce, proclamation, and plebiscite.[74]

During the second half of the nineteenth century, independence was associated with sovereignty and hence with juridical status rather than with national identities, whether ethnic, linguistic, historical, or religious. Nationalism was a force for consolidation and aggregation in emerging nation-states like Germany and Italy; declarations of independence were indexes of fragmentation and separation which betrayed centrifugal forces that ran counter to the centripetal pull of nation-formation. Moreover, the heyday of European nationalism coincided with the zenith of extra-European imperialism. As nation-states consolidated within Europe, so they extended their imperial holdings beyond it: in this sense, "Europe in the 1870s was not a Europe of nation-states but of empires, old and would-be."[75]

The forces behind both consolidation and expansion were antithetical to the impulses that had led before 1850, and would lead again after 1918, to declarations of independence.[76] An Asian counter-example to this generalization may suffice to illustrate the different definitions of sovereignty available in the late nineteenth century. A short-lived Taiwanese republic was proclaimed in May 1895, partly to prevent a Japanese takeover of the island after the first Sino-Japanese War (1894–1895). The contemporary American translator of the document that announced the republic termed it the "Official Declaration of the Republic of Formosa," but it is clear that this was a misunderstanding of the nature of the claim to autonomy made by the leaders of the short-lived Taiwanese republic. Those who proclaimed that republic appealed to western powers for help, something which could be achieved only if Taiwan were recognized internationally as autonomous. However, this did not necessarily imply complete separation from China. The Taiwan Republic was proclaimed to be "self-dependent," not "independent," *(duli)* from China, and its president, Tang Jingsong, presented himself to the people of Taiwan as a loyal servant of the Qing emperor. He therefore did not claim full international sovereignty for Taiwan: thus, "this first Asian republic did not arise as a product of a revolution or the outcome of an independence movement."[77] In contrast, the next Asian republic, Mongolia, would in fact arise from revolution in 1911, when, with the imminent collapse of the Qing dynasty, the assembled khans proclaimed "to the Mongols, Russians, Tibetans, Chinese and all ecclesiastical and secular commoners" the resumption of their historic independence and their resolution no longer to be ruled by "Manchu-Chinese officials."[78]

The twentieth century witnessed two great heydays of declaring independence: one in the immediate aftermath of the First World War; the other, beginning in 1945 and continuing until 1993, with a short hiatus in the 1970s and early 1980s. The collapse of the great European land empires during and after the First World War led to the re-emergence of submerged nationalities from these prisons of nations and to the creation of new states to accommodate them, often with the accompaniment of a declaration of independence. In this period, the declaration most clearly indebted to the American example was the "Declaration of Independence of the Czechoslovak Nation" (October 18, 1918). This document was drafted in Washington, D.C., by Tomas Masaryk (in Czech) and revised (in English) by, among others, Gutzon Borglum, the sculptor of Mount Rushmore. It placed the American Declaration within a lineage stretching from the proto-Protestantism of Jan Hus in the fifteenth century all the way to the Wilsonian promise of self-determination in the early twentieth.[79]

Masaryk was clearly appealing for American support with these allusions: as he put it in an article in *The Nation,* "the Czecho-Slovak nation invokes the principles of the Declaration of Independence for its revolution. . . . The United States cannot accept Austrianism, for it is a denial and a contradiction of the Declaration of Independence and of American ideals."[80] A week after the Czech declaration, Masaryk presided over the composition of a more sweepingly general "Declaration of Independence of the Mid-European Union" (October 26, 1918) in Philadelphia, which he signed using the Philip Syng inkwell used by the signers of the American Declaration in 1776.[81]

Similar appeals to the promise of self-determination animated many other declarations of independence from this period, including the "Proclamation of the State of the Slovenes, Croats, and Serbs" (October 29, 1918), the Dáil Éireann's Irish declaration of independence (January 21, 1919), the Korean declaration of independence (March 1, 1919), and Estonia's declaration of independence (May 19, 1919).[82] It was also during this period that an anticolonial movement against the British concertedly deployed the revolutionary language of the American Declaration for the first time since 1776. In January 1930, Mahatma Gandhi drafted a declaration for the Indian National Congress stating "the inalienable right of the Indian people . . . to have freedom and to enjoy the fruits of their toil and have the necessities of life, so that they may have full opportunities of growth. We believe also that if any government deprives a people of these rights and oppresses them, the people have a further right to alter it or to abolish it." On these grounds, Gandhi argued, "we believe . . . that India must sever

the British connection and attain *purna* swaraj or complete independence," though he soon clarified his statement: the document was "*not* to declare independence but to declare that we
will be satisfied with nothing less than complete independence
as opposed to Dominion Status so-called."[83] Subhas Chandra
Bose later proclaimed the first independent Indian government
of Azad Hind (Free India) in October 21, 1943, from Singa-
pore. Like the American Congress, Bose's Provisional Government declared independence in order to gain foreign recognition for an armed struggle against the British Empire. It was
thus no accident that he did so with language drawn from the
American Declaration, "pledg[ing] our lives and the lives of our
comrades-in-arms to the cause of [India's] Freedom, of her
Welfare, and her exaltation among the nations of the world,"
and declaring his government's "firm resolve to pursue the happiness of the whole nation and all its parts."[84]

    The anticolonial declaration from this moment most clearly
patterned on the American Declaration would be Ho Chi Minh's
Vietnamese declaration of independence, issued in the immediate aftermath of the collapse of the French empire in Indochina
in 1945. It opened with quotations from the second paragraph
of the American Declaration (which Ho had checked with
the American OSS officer Archimedes Patti) and the French
Declaration of the Rights of Man and the Citizen.[85] The Vietnamese declaration continued with a list of grievances against

French colonialism probably patterned after the charges against the king in the American Declaration. Like the American example, it spoke to both domestic audiences (for whom independence was effectively a *fait accompli*) and foreign observers (from whom Vietnam desired international recognition). Ho, long an admirer of George Washington, thereby placed the Vietnamese revolution into a longer revolutionary tradition while also making a shrewd bid for American support for Vietnamese independence, retrospectively from Japan and prospectively from France.[86] However, "by October 1945, it was clear that the only people ready to recognize the freedom and independence of Vietnam were the Vietnamese people themselves."[87]

The late twentieth-century document most closely modeled on the language of the American Declaration would be the example that clarified, once and for all, the terms on which any such declaration could be recognized by the international community. This was the Unilateral Declaration of Independence (UDI) issued by the embattled white minority government of Southern Rhodesia on November 11, 1965. In conscious imitation of the 1776 Declaration, it opened with the words, "Whereas in the course of human affairs history has shown that it may become necessary for a people to resolve the political affiliations which have connected them with another people and to assume among other nations the separate and equal status to which they are entitled . . ."[88] The document included no references to individual rights, however. Both sides in the Rhodesian dispute between Ian Smith's minority regime and the British government understood the confrontation with the elephantine memory of imperial elites as a re-run of the American Revolution. In March 1963, more than two years before UDI, Harold Macmillan's Conservative government had investigated military contingency plans against the possibility of Rhodesian independence: the ominous title of the secret file containing the resulting documents was "Boston Tea Party."[89]

The Rhodesian Declaration appeared only five years after the United Nations issued its Declaration on the Granting of Independence to Colonial Countries and Peoples (1960). In this document, the United Nations proclaimed that "the process of liberation is irresistible and irreversible," and that "all peoples"—meaning all majority peoples—"have an inalienable right to complete freedom, the exercise of their sovereignty and the integrity of their national territory."[90] Because the Rhodesian Declaration did not reflect the democratically determined right to freedom and sovereignty of the majority population of Rhodesia, it provided no legitimate basis for recognizing the independence of the government that had promulgated it.[91]

As the Rhodesian example showed, the criteria for legitimate state creation had developed considerably since 1776. Declarations of independence like those of Liberia and Hungary appealed to a standard of civilization shared by other

states in Europe and the Atlantic world. After both Lenin and
Woodrow Wilson had proclaimed their conceptions of self-
determination in the closing years of the First World War, that
concept became a standard around which secessionist movements—like that in Czechoslavakia—could rally. After the Second World War, the United Nations would come to be an arbiter of international norms, as the appeal to a UN Resolution,
among other sources, in the Declaration of the Establishment of
the State of Israel (May 14, 1948) showed. The spread of rights-
talk since 1948 and the Universal Declaration of Human Rights
have only increased international pressure to bring structures of
internal sovereignty into harmony with the mechanisms of external sovereignty, just as they helped to accelerate the movement toward decolonization since the Second World War.

Since 1776, declarations of independence have been primarily assertions of sovereignty, both externally, against any colo-
nizing or occupying power, and internally, as they have defined
a new state's source of legitimacy, its claim to territory, and its
assertion of international legal personality. The dilemmas resulting from the contagion of sovereignty that this fact repre-
sents can be traced back at least as far as the American Revolution. They cannot be traced back much further than that,
however, because the association between independence and
statehood was quite novel at the moment Americans declared
their independence from Great Britain in 1776.

Some observers have argued that the Americas, starting with

British North America in 1776, were not a nursery of nations, far in advance of the springtime of nations that emerged in the second part of the nineteenth century. However, as this examination of the Declaration of Independence and its successors has shown, the western hemisphere in the Age of Revolutions might best be considered a crucible of states: "the validity and generalizability of the blueprint were undoubtedly confirmed by the *plurality* of the independent states."[92] Thus it would be no exaggeration to say that the origins of our modern world of states can be traced back to the Americas and, in particular, to the American Revolution. The political theorist Hannah Arendt lamented: "The sad truth of the matter is that the French Revolution, which ended in disaster, has made world history, while the American Revolution, so triumphantly successful, has remained an event of little more than local importance."[93] On the contrary: the American Revolution was an event of truly global importance. Its contagious consequences spread to encompass the entire world of states we all now inhabit for good and ill but, for the time being, inescapably.

Conclusion

This history of the Declaration of Independence has traced the international origins and global afterlives of a single pointed and eclectic document. Its findings should be set alongside the recent judgment of one leading historian of the American Revolution that the "Declaration set forth a philosophy of human rights that could be applied not only to Americans but to peoples everywhere. It was essential in giving the American Revolution a universal appeal."[1] The story I have told here concerns the rights of states more than the rights of individuals, and the claims to recognition of communities within the international realm rather than the claims of citizens or subjects against their rulers. These two assessments are not necessarily incompatible.

The Declaration spoke both of the rights of free and independent states and of the rights of "all Men" to "Life, Liberty, and the Pursuit of Happiness." Part of its appeal, both within the United States and in the wider world, lay in its incorporation of both species of rights within its argument. But the greater prominence of the Declaration's assertions of statehood in the history of its global reception and imitation accurately reflects the intentions of its authors and better describes the balance of its intended argument.

No document's meaning can be entirely constrained by the intentions of its creators. This is especially true of a document, like the Declaration, that comes to be seen as the beginning of a genre. Thomas Jefferson's achievement in 1776 was to use his forensic and rhetorical skill to forge an instrument for declaring independence without any earlier models to guide him. Later revolutionaries, secessionists, and separatists would have no need to make such a creative leap, as over time the number of models available to inspire their declarations would multiply and diversify. With proliferation and variegation would also come more vivid revelations of the competing imperatives at the heart of the Declaration itself, between peoples and states, and between the individual bearers of rights and the sovereigns who claimed their own rights against other sovereigns. For these reasons, what made the Declaration so attractive around the world—its combination of appeals to natural rights and positive law, its eclectic suspension of personal and corporate rights, and its amalgam of the elements of what would become discrete genres of political argument—also make its afterlife a revealing index of major dilemmas within world history since 1776.

Declarations of independence were primarily assertions of external sovereignty within an expanding universe of other such sovereigns. They were the peculiar products of an era in which states were increasingly identified as the primary units of world politics and as other, competing political forms were gradually retreating from the world stage: thus, no state now officially calls itself an empire, even though some have analysts or cheerleaders for their policies who unofficially use the language of empire on their behalf. Over the past two centuries, the criteria for the recognition of sovereignty by other states have changed dramatically. The genre of a declaration of independence has been sufficiently flexible to include appeals to Vattelian definitions of statehood, the language of "civilization," Wilsonian conceptions of self-determination, and the burgeoning discourse of human rights, for example. Just how compatible all these appeals are with the assertion of state sovereignty internationally remains one of the unresolved questions of the contemporary global order.

The intractability of that dilemma becomes particularly clear in the fundamental ambivalence of independence itself. It seems to be a historical rule that once states have established their own independence they become resistant to further internal challenges to their autonomy or integrity: "In such cases, the right reverses into a taboo."[2] That ambivalence became evident as early as 1777, when the United States resisted the independence of Vermont. Almost the only major exception to the rule since the Second World War has been Bangladesh, which seceded from Pakistan in 1971 with an accompanying proclamation of independence, though not without great bloodshed in the passage to statehood.[3] Independent states resist further claims to independence mostly because territoriality links independence to statehood: without a defined territory, there can be no state, and without a state there can be no meaningful independence, runs the equation. Territoriality has long been the stubborn heart of statehood: when two peoples claim the same territory, their irreconcilable declarations of independence can vie for validation, as in the case of Israel and Palestine.[4]

As long as sovereignty confined within statehood remained the presumed end-point of self-determination, there was little hope for many internal minorities—especially indigenous peoples—to obtain independence under reigning definitions of the term. The New Zealand declaration of independence (1835) illustrated this bleak conclusion when it declared independence on behalf of indigenous groups only as the basis for a reduction in their autonomy by agents of the British Crown. Increasingly, indigenous peoples have resorted to instruments other than declarations of independence to secure their rights and claim autonomy.[5]

Such a strategic shift may indicate that declarations of independence will never again be as prolific as they have been in the past. Groups seeking to promote their cause may now choose other forms of self-determination—such as devolution, condominium, and more extensive political representation—which do not make claims to territory or to admission "among the Powers of the Earth." There are, of course, counter-examples to such a generalization, as there will surely be disconfirmations of any prediction so sweeping in its scope. Though the legal assessments of recent movements, such as the movement for Québécois separatism, have denied the existence of a presumptive right to secession by any province or people, that does not entail that no attempts at secession will be made, even in the teeth of prevailing international legal norms and the resistance of existing states. It is not hard to imagine a series of challenges to the seventeenth- and eighteenth-century Qing empire that is the territorial heart of the Chinese state, further fragmentation of the Russian Federation (as in Chechnya), or more vigorous separatist agitations in Indonesia or India, for example. Whether they will be accompanied by declarations of independence remains to be seen. Within our all-enveloping world of stubbornly sovereign territorial entities, there may be few remaining opportunities for successful declarations of independent statehood. Even in such a world, the Declaration will remain "an instrument, pregnant with [Americans'] own and the fate of the world," not for the reasons Jefferson might have hoped but because of consequences he could not have foreseen.

Declarations of Independence, 1776–1993

The table that follows lists the numerous declarations of independence that have appeared since 1776. Wherever possible, I have listed sources for full texts of the declarations as well as for translations (where relevant). A selection of sample texts appears after the table.

Abbreviations

Actas	*Las Actas de Independencia de América,* ed. Javier Malagón (Washington, D.C., 1955)
BFSP	*British and Foreign State Papers,* 170 vols. (London, 1841–1977)
IDOW	*Independence Documents of the World,* ed. Albert P. Blaustein, Jay Sigler, and Benjamin R. Beede, 2 vols. (New York, 1977)
TNA	The National Archives, Kew, United Kingdom

Year	State	Date	Source
1776	United States	July 4	*The Papers of Thomas Jefferson,* gen. eds. Julian P. Boyd et al., 31 vols. to date (Princeton, 1950–), I, 429–432
1777	Vermont	Jan. 15	*Records of the Council of Safety and Governor and Council of the State of Vermont,* ed. E. P. Walton, 8 vols. (Montpelier, VT, 1873–1880), I, 40–44
1790	Flanders	Jan. 4	J. F. Rohaert, *Manifeste de la Province de Flandre* (Ghent, 1790)
1804	Haïti	Jan. 1	Thomas Madiou, *Histoire d'Haïti,* 8 vols. (Port-au-Prince, 1989–1991), III, 146–150; Marcus Rainsford, *An Historical Account of the Black Empire of Hayti* (London, 1805), 442–446

Year	State	Date	Source
1810	Colombia	July 20	*Actas*, 26–28
1811	Venezuela	July 5	*Historia y comentarios del libro de actas de la independencia de Venezuela 1811*, ed. P. L. Blanco Peñalver (Caracas, 1983), 41–46; *Interesting Official Documents Relating to the United Provinces of Venezuela* (London, 1812), 2–21
1811	New Granada	Nov. 11	*Documentos para la historia de la vida pública del libertador de Colombia, Péru y Bolivia*, ed. José Félix Blanco, 14 vols. (Caracas, 1875–1877), III, 357–360; *BFSP*, 1 (1812–1814), 1136–1142
1813	Mexico	Nov. 6	Carlos María de Bustamente, *Cuadro historíco de la revolucíon mexicana*, 5 vols. (Mexico, 1843–1846), II, 406–407
1816	Argentina	July 9	*Registro Oficial de la República Argentina*, 14 vols. (Buenos Aires, 1879–1891), I, 366; *BFSP*, 5 (1817–1818), 804
1818	Chile	Jan. 1	*Documentos para la historia de la vida pública del libertador*, ed. Blanco, VI, 238–239; *BFSP*, 6 (1818–1819), 820–821
1821	Peru	July 28	*Documentos para la historia de la vida pública del libertador*, ed. Blanco, VIII, 5–7; *BFSP*, 9 (1821–1822), 393–394

Year	State	Date	Source
1821	Guatemala	Sept. 15	*Documentos para la historia de la vida pública del libertador,* ed. Blanco, VIII, 67–68
1821	El Salvador	Sept. 21	*Textos Fundamentales de la Independencia Centroamericana,* ed. Carlos Meléndez (San José, Costa Rica, 1971), 266–268
1821	Mexico	Sept. 28	*El Libertador: Documentos Selectos de D. Agustín de Iturbide,* ed. Mariano Cuevas (Mexico City, 1947), 262–263; *IDOW,* II, 471–476
1821	Nicaragua	Sept. 28	*Textos Fundamentales de la Independencia Centroamericana,* ed. Meléndez, 274
1821	Costa Rica	Oct. 29	*Textos Fundamentales de la Independencia Centroamericana,* ed. Meléndez, 282–283
1821	Panama	Nov. 28	*Actas,* 88
1822	Hellenic Republic	Jan. 27	John L. Comstock, *History of the Greek Revolution* (New York, 1828), 499–500
1822	Brazil	Sept. 7	*A Documentary History of Brazil,* ed. E. Bradford Burns (New York, 1956), 199–200
1823	Nicaragua	July 1	*Actas,* 83–84
1823	United Provinces of Central America	July 11	*Textos Fundamentales de la Independencia Centroamericana,* ed. Meléndez, 420–424; *IDOW,* I, 142–145

Year	State	Date	Source
1825	Bolivia	Aug. 6	*Documentos para la historia de la vida pública del libertador,* ed. Blanco, X, 62–65; *BFSP,* 13 (1825–1826), 859–862
1825	Uruguay	Aug. 25	Antonio T. Caravia, *Collecion de leyes, decretos y resoluciones gubernativas . . . de la república oriental de Uruguay,* 3 vols. (Montevideo, 1867), I, 13–14; *IDOW,* I, 744
1830	Ecuador	May 13	*IDOW,* I, 200–201
1830	Belgium	Oct. 4	*BFSP,* 17 (1829–1830), 1232
1831	Colombia	Nov. 21	*BFSP,* 18 (1830–1831), 1359–1360
1835	New Zealand	Oct. 28	*Fac-Similes of the Declaration of Independence and the Treaty of Waitangi* (Wellington, NZ, 1877), 4
1836	Texas	March 2	*The Papers of the Texas Revolution, 1835–1836,* gen. ed. John H. Jenkins, 9 vols. (Austin, 1973), IV, 493–497
1836	Alta California	Nov. 7 (not recognized)	[Parke-Bernet Galleries,] *The Celebrated Collection of Americana Formed by the Late Thomas Streeter, Morristown, New Jersey,* 8 vols. (New York, 1968), IV, 1781
1838	Nicaragua	April 30	*IDOW,* I, 522
1838	Honduras	Oct. 26	*IDOW,* I, 329

Year	State	Date	Source
1838	Costa Rica	May 30	*IDOW*, I, 146–147
1842	Paraguay	Nov. 25	*Actas*, 98–99; *BFSP*, 34 (1845–1846), 1320–1321
1844	Dominican Republic	Jan. 16	Emilio Rodríguez Demorizi, *El acta de la separación Dominicana y el acta de independencia de los Estados Unidos de America* (Ciudad Trujillo, 1943), 33–46
1847	Liberia	July 26	*The Independent Republic of Liberia; Its Constitution and Declaration of Independence* (Philadelphia, 1848), 8–9
1849	Hungary	April 14	*Kossuth Lajos összes munkái,* 15 vols. (Budapest, 1948–1966), XIV, 894–912; William H. Stiles, *Austria in 1848–49,* 2 vols. (New York, 1852), II, 409–418
1860	South Carolina	Dec. 20	*Journal of the Convention of the People of South Carolina, Held in 1860, 1861 and 1862* (Columbia, SC, 1862), 461–466
1895	Taiwan	May 23	James W. Davidson, *The Island of Formosa Past and Present* (Yokohama, 1903), 279–281
1898	Philippines	June 12	John R. M. Taylor, *The Philippine Insurrection against the United States,* 5 vols. (Pasay City, 1971), III, 102–106
1903	Panama	Nov. 4	*Actas*, 90
1908	Bulgaria	Sept. 22	*IDOW*, I, 94–95

Year	State	Date	Source
1911	Mongolia	Dec. 1	Urgunge Onon and Derrick Pritchatt, *Asia's First Modern Revolution: Mongolia Proclaims Its Independence in 1911* (Leiden, 1989), 126
1917	Finland	Dec. 6	*IDOW*, I, 228–230
1918	Lithuania	Feb. 16	
1918	Estonia	Feb. 24	
1918	Czechoslovakia	Oct. 18	George J. Kovtun, *The Czechoslovak Declaration of Independence: A History of the Document* (Washington, D.C., 1985), 53–55
1918	Latvia	Nov. 18	
1918	Georgia	May 26	
1918	Yugoslavia	Oct. 29	*Yugoslavia through Documents: From Its Creation to Its Dissolution,* ed. Snezana Trifunovska (Dordrecht, 1994), 147–148
1919	Republic of Ireland	Jan. 21	*Ireland's Declaration of Independence and Other Official Documents* (New York, 1919), 3
1919	Korea	March 1	"The Declaration of Independence, March 1, 1919: A New Translation," *Korean Studies,* 13 (1989), 1–4
1919	Estonia	May 19	TNA, FO 608/186, fols. 229–230
1941	Syria	Sept. 27	*IDOW*, II, 679–680
1943	Yugoslavia	Nov. 29	*IDOW*, II, 784–790

Year	State	Date	Source
1944	Iceland	June 16	*IDOW,* I, 334
1945	Austria	April 27	*Red-White-Red Book: Justice for Austria* (Vienna, 1947), 211–212
1945	Indonesia	Aug. 17	*IDOW,* I, 342–343
1945	Vietnam	Sept. 2	Ho Chi Minh, *Selected Works,* 4 vols. (Hanoi, 1960–1962), III, 17–21
1948	Israel	May 14	*IDOW,* I, 371
1950	South Moluccas	April 25 (not recognized)	Clive J. Christie, *A Modern History of Southeast Asia: Decolonization, Nationalism and Separatism* (London, 1996), 224
1951	Libya	Dec. 24	*IDOW,* II, 428–429
1957	Malaysia	August 31	*IDOW,* II, 449–451
1958	Guinea	Oct. 2	*IDOW,* I, 300–302
1960	Togo	April 23	*IDOW,* II, 700
1960	Democratic Republic of Congo (Zaire)	June 30	
1960	Katanga	July 11 (not recognized)	Jules Gérard-Libois, *Katanga Secession,* trans. Rebecca Young (Madison, 1966), 328–329
1960	Dahomey (Benin)	Aug. 1	
1960	Niger	Aug. 6	*IDOW,* II, 526
1960	Senegal	Aug. 25	
1960	Mali	Sept. 22	*IDOW,* II, 458–459
1960	Mauritania	Oct. 19	*IDOW,* II, 465
1961	Rwanda	Jan. 28	*IDOW,* II, 594–595
1961	Tanganyika	Nov. 22	

Year	State	Date	Source
1965	Singapore	Aug. 7	*IDOW,* II, 620–622
1965	Southern Rhodesia	Nov. 11 (not recognized)	*IDOW,* II, 587
1967	Biafra	May 30	Chukwuemeka Odumegwu Ojukwu, *Ahiara Declaration: The Principles of the Biafran Revolution* (June 1, 1969) (Glenn Dale, 2003), 51–52
1968	Equatorial Guinea	Oct. 12	*IDOW,* I, 218
1971	Bangladesh	April 10	*Bangla Desh: Documents* (New Delhi, [1971?]), 281–282
1971	Bahrain	Aug. 14	*IDOW,* I, 46–50
1971	United Arab Emirates	Dec. 1	*IDOW,* II, 722–723
1973	Guinea-Bissau	Sept. 24	*IDOW,* II, 307–310
1975	Angola	Nov. 11	*Angola: Documentos de Independência* (Lisbon, 1976), 7–20
1975	East Timor	Nov. 28	Jill Jolliffe, *East Timor: Nationalism and Colonialism* (St Lucia, Qld., 1978), 212
1983	Turkish Republic of Northern Cyprus	Nov. 15 (not recognized)	UN Doc. A/38/586–S/16148
1988	Palestine National Council	Nov. 15 (not recognized)	*The Israel-Arab Reader: A Documentary of the Middle East Conflict,* ed. Walter Laqueur and Barry Rubin, 6th ed. (Harmondsworth, 2001), 354–357

Year	State	Date	Source
1990	Lithuania	March 11	
1991	Uzbekistan		
1991	Georgia	April 9	
1991	Slovenia	June 25	*Yugoslavia through Documents,* ed. Trifunovska, 286–290
1991	Croatia	June 25	*Yugoslavia through Documents,* ed. Trifunovska, 301–304
1991	Estonia	Aug. 20	
1991	Latvia	Aug. 21	
1991	Ukraine	Aug. 24	
1991	Belarus	Aug. 25	
1991	Moldova	Aug. 27	
1991	Azerbaijan	Aug. 30	
1991	Uzbekistan	Aug. 31	
1991	Kyrgyzstan	Aug. 31	
1991	Nagorno-Karabakh	Sept. 3 (not recognized)	
1991	Crimea	Sept. 4	
1991	Tajikistan	Sept. 9	
1991	Macedonia	Sept. 17	*Yugoslavia through Documents,* ed. Trifunovska, 345–347
1991	Republic of Kosovo	Sept. 22	*The Crisis in Kosovo, 1989–1999* (Cambridge, 1999), 72
1991	Armenia	Sept. 23	
1991	Turkmenistan	Oct. 27	
1991	Chechnya	Nov. 2	
1991	South Ossetia	Nov. 28	
1991	Kazakhstan	Dec. 16	
1991	Serb Republic of Krajina	Dec. 19	

Year	State	Date	Source
1992	Bosnia-Herzegovina	March 3	
1992	Tatarstan	March 21	
1992	Serbian Republic of Bosnia and Herzegovina	April 7	
1992	Crimea	May 5 (not recognized)	
1992	Republika Srpska	July 4 (not recognized)	
1992	Abkhazia	July 24 (not recognized)	
1993	Eritrea	May 24	

Thomas Jefferson's "Original Rough Draft" of the Declaration of Independence

A Declaration of the Representatives of the
UNITED STATES OF AMERICA, in General Congress assembled.

When in the course of human events it becomes necessary for a people to advance from that subordination in which they have hitherto remained, & to assume among the powers of the earth the equal & independant station to which the laws of nature & of nature's god entitle them, a decent respect to the opinions of mankind requires that they should declare the causes which impel them to the change.

We hold these truths to be sacred & undeniable; that all men are created equal & independant, that from that equal creation they derive rights inherent & inalienable, among which are the preservation of life, & liberty, & the pursuit of happiness; that to secure these ends, governments are instituted among men, deriving their just powers from the consent of the governed; that whenever any form of government shall become destructive of these ends, it is the right of the people to alter or to abolish it, & to institute new government, laying it's foundation on such principles & organising it's powers in such form, as to them shall seem most likely to effect their safety & happiness. prudence indeed will dictate that governments long established should not be changed for light & transient causes: and accordingly all experience hath shewn that mankind are more disposed to suffer while evils are sufferable, than to right themselves by abolishing the forms to which they are accustomed. but when a long train of abuses & usurpations, begun at a distinguished period, & pursuing invariably the same object, evinces a design to subject them to arbitrary power, it is their right, it is their duty, to throw off such government & to provide new guards for their future security. such has been the patient sufferance of these colonies; & such is now the necessity which constrains them to expunge their former systems of government. the history of his present majesty, is a history of unremitting injuries and usurpations, among which no one fact stands single or solitary to contradict the uniform tenor of the rest, all of which have in direct object the establishment of an absolute tyranny over these states. to prove this, let facts be submitted to a candid world, for the truth of which we pledge a faith yet unsullied by falsehood.

he has refused his assent to laws the most wholesome and necessary for the public good:

he has forbidden his governors to pass laws of immediate &

pressing importance, unless suspended in their operation till his assent should be obtained; and when so suspended, he has neglected utterly to attend to them.

he has refused to pass other laws for the accomodation of large districts of people unless those people would relinquish the right of representation, a right inestimable to them, & formidable to tyrants alone:

he has dissolved Representative houses repeatedly & continually, for opposing with manly firmness his invasions on the rights of the people:

he has refused for a long space of time to cause others to be elected, whereby the legislative powers, incapable of annihilation, have returned to the people at large for their exercise, the state remaining in the mean time exposed to all the dangers of invasion from without, & convulsions within:

he has endeavored to prevent the population of these states; for that purpose obstructing the laws for naturalization of foreigners; refusing to pass others to encourage their migrations hither; & raising the conditions of new appropriations of lands:

he has suffered the administration of justice totally to cease in some of these colonies, refusing his assent to laws for establishing judiciary powers:

he has made our judges dependant on his will alone, for the tenure of their offices, and amount of their salaries:

he has erected a multitude of new offices by a self-assumed power, & sent hither swarms of officers to harrass our people & eat out their substance:

he has kept among us in times of peace standing armies & ships of war:

he has affected to render the military, independant of & superior to the civil power:

he has combined with others to subject us to a jurisdiction foreign to our constitutions and unacknoleged by our laws; giving his assent to their pretended acts of legislation, for quartering large bodies of armed troops among us;

for protecting them by a mock-trial from punishment for any murders they should commit on the inhabitants of these states;

for cutting off our trade with all parts of the world;

for imposing taxes on us without our consent;

for depriving us of the benefits of trial by jury;

for transporting us beyond seas to be tried for pretended offences:

for taking away our charters, & altering fundamentally the forms of our governments;

for suspending our own legislatures & declaring themselves invested with power to legislate for us in all cases whatsoever:

he has abdicated government here, withdrawing his governors, & declaring us out of his allegiance & protection:

he has plundered our seas, ravaged our coasts, burnt our towns & destroyed the lives of our people:

he is at this time transporting large armies of foreign mercenaries to compleat the works of death, desolation & tyranny, already begun with circumstances of cruelty & perfidy unworthy the head of a civilized nation:

he has endeavored to bring on the inhabitants of our frontiers the merciless Indian savages, whose known rule of warfare is an undistinguished destruction of all ages, sexes, & conditions of existence:

he has incited treasonable insurrections in our fellow-subjects, with the allurements of forfeiture & confiscation of our property:

he has waged cruel war against human nature itself, violating it's most sacred rights of life & liberty in the persons of a distant people who never offended him, captivating & carrying them into slavery in another hemisphere, or to incur miserable death in their transportation thither. this piratical warfare, the opprobrium of *infidel* powers, is the warfare of the CHRISTIAN king of Great Britain. determined to keep open a market where MEN should be bought & sold, he has prostituted his negative for suppressing every legislative attempt to prohibit or to restrain this execrable commerce: and that this assemblage of horrors might want no fact of distinguished die, he is now exciting those very people to rise in arms among us, and to purchase that liberty of which *he* has deprived them, by murdering the people upon whom *he* also obtruded them; thus paying off former crimes committed against the *liberties* of one people, with crimes which he urges them to commit against the *lives* of another.

in every stage of these oppressions we have petitioned for redress in the most humble terms; our repeated petitions have been answered by repeated injury. a prince whose character is thus marked by every act which may define a tyrant, is unfit to be the ruler of a people who mean to be free. future ages will scarce believe that the hardiness of one man, adventured within the short compass of 12 years only, on so many acts of tyranny without a mask, over a people fostered & fixed in principles of liberty.

Nor have we been wanting in attentions to our British brethren. we have warned them from time to time of attempts by their legislature to extend a jurisdiction over these our states. we have reminded them of the circumstances of our emigration & settlement here, no one of which could warrant so strange a pretension: that these were effected at the expence of our own blood & treasure, unassisted by the wealth or the strength of Great Britain: that in constituting indeed our several forms of government, we had adopted one common king, thereby laying a foundation for perpetual league & amity with them: but that submission to their parliament was no part of our constitution, nor ever in idea, if history may be credited: and we appealed to their native justice & magnanimity, as well as to the ties of our common kindred to disavow these usurpations which were likely to interrupt our correspondence & connection. they too have been deaf to the voice of justice & of consanguinity, & when occasions have been given them, by the regular course of their laws, of removing from their councils the disturbers of our harmony, they have by their free election re-established them in power. at this very time too they are permitting their chief magistrate to send over not only soldiers of our common blood, but Scotch & foreign mercenaries to invade & deluge us in blood. these facts have given the last stab to agonizing affection, and manly spirit bids us to renounce for ever these unfeeling brethren. we must endeavor to forget our former love for them, and to hold them as we hold the rest of mankind, enemies in war, in peace friends. we might have been a free & a great people together; but a communication of grandeur & of freedom it seems is below their dignity. be it so, since they will have it: the road to glory & happiness is open to us too; we will climb it in a separate state, and acquiesce in the necessity which pronounces our everlasting Adieu!

We therefore the representatives of the United States of America in General Congress assembled do, in the name & by authority of the good people of these states, reject and renounce all allegiance & subjection to the kings of Great Britain & all others who may hereafter claim by, through, or under them; we utterly dissolve & break off all political connection which may have heretofore subsisted between us & the people or parliament of Great Britain; and finally we do assert and declare these colonies to be free and independant states, and that as free & independant states they shall hereafter have power to levy war, conclude peace, contract alliances, establish commerce, & to do all other acts and things which independant states may of right do. And for the support of this declaration we mutually pledge to each other our lives, our fortunes, & our sacred honour

---

Source: The Papers of Thomas Jefferson, gen. eds. Julian P. Boyd et al., 31 vols. to date (Princeton, 1950–), I, 423–427.

In Congress, July 4, 1776.
A Declaration By the Representatives of the United
States of America, in General Congress Assembled

When in the Course of human Events, it becomes necessary for one People to dissolve the Political Bands which have connected them with another, and to assume among the Powers of the Earth, the separate and equal Station to which the Laws of Nature and of Nature's God entitle them, a decent Respect to the Opinions of Mankind requires that they should declare the causes which impel them to the Separation.

We hold these Truths to be self-evident, that all Men are created equal, that they are endowed by their Creator with certain unalienable Rights, that among these are Life, Liberty, and the Pursuit of Happiness—That to secure these Rights, Governments are instituted among Men, deriving their just Powers from the Consent of the Governed, that whenever any Form of Government becomes destructive of these Ends, it is the Right of the People to alter or to abolish it, and to institute new Government, laying its Foundation on such Principles, and organizing its Powers in such Form, as to them shall seem most likely to effect their Safety and Happiness. Prudence, indeed, will dictate that Governments long established should not be changed for light and transient Causes; and accordingly all Experience hath shewn, that Mankind are more disposed to suffer, while Evils are sufferable, than to right themselves by abolishing the Forms to which they are accustomed. But when a long Train of Abuses and Usurpations, pursuing invariably the same Object, evinces a Design to reduce them under absolute Despotism, it is their Right, it is their Duty, to throw off such Government, and to provide new Guards for their future Security. Such has been the patient Sufferance of these Colonies; and such is now the Necessity which constrains them to alter their former Systems of Government. The History of the present King of Great-Britain is a History of repeated Injuries and Usurpations, all having in direct Object the Establishment of an absolute Tyranny over these States. To prove this, let Facts be submitted to a candid World.

He has refused his Assent to Laws, the most wholesome and necessary for the public Good.

He has forbidden his Governors to pass Laws of immediate and pressing Importance, unless suspended in their Operation till his Assent should be obtained; and when so suspended, he has utterly neglected to attend to them.

He has refused to pass other Laws for the Accommodation of large Districts of People, unless those People would relinquish the Right of Representation in the Legislature, a Right inestimable to them and formidable to Tyrants only.

He has called together Legislative Bodies at Places unusual, uncomfortable, and distant from the Depository of their public Records, for the sole Purpose of fatiguing them into Compliance with his Measures.

He has dissolved Representative Houses repeatedly, for opposing with manly Firmness his Invasions on the Rights of the People.

He has refused for a long Time, after such Dissolutions, to cause others to be elected; whereby the Legislative Powers, incapable of Annihilation, have returned to the People at large for their exercise; the State remaining in the mean time exposed to all the Dangers of Invasion from without, and Convulsions within.

He has endeavoured to prevent the Population of these States; for that Purpose obstructing the Laws for Naturalization of Foreigners; refusing to pass others to encourage their Migrations hither, and raising the Conditions of new Appropriations of Lands.

He has obstructed the Administration of Justice, by refusing his Assent to Laws for establishing Judiciary Powers.

He has made Judges dependent on his Will alone, for the Tenure of their Offices, and the Amount and Payment of their Salaries.

He has erected a Multitude of new Offices, and sent hither Swarms of Officers to harrass our People, and eat out their Substance.

He has kept among us, in Times of Peace, Standing Armies without the Consent of our Legislatures.

He has affected to render the Military independent of and superior to the Civil Power.

He has combined with others to subject us to a Jurisdiction foreign to our Constitution, and unacknowledged by our Laws; giving his Assent to their Acts of pretended Legislation:

For quartering large Bodies of Armed Troops among us:

For protecting them, by a mock Trial, from Punishment for any Murders which they should commit on the Inhabitants of these States:

For cutting off our Trade with all Parts of the World:

For imposing Taxes on us without our Consent:

For depriving us, in many Cases, of the Benefits of Trial by Jury:

For transporting us beyond Seas to be tried for pretended Offences:

For abolishing the free System of English Laws in a neighbouring Province, establishing therein an arbitrary Government, and enlarging its Boundaries, so as to render it at once an Example and fit Instrument for introducing the same absolute Rule into these Colonies:

For taking away our Charters, abolishing our most valuable Laws, and altering fundamentally the Forms of our Governments:

For suspending our own Legislatures, and declaring themselves invested with Power to legislate for us in all Cases whatsoever.

He has abdicated Government here, by declaring us out of his Protection and waging War against us.

He has plundered our Seas, ravaged our Coasts, burnt our Towns, and destroyed the Lives of our People.

He is, at this Time, transporting large Armies of foreign Mercenaries to compleat the Works of Death, Desolation, and Tyranny, already begun with circumstances of Cruelty and Perfidy, scarcely paralleled in the most barbarous Ages, and totally unworthy the Head of a civilized Nation.

He has constrained our fellow Citizens taken Captive on the high Seas to bear Arms against their Country, to become the Executioners of their Friends and Brethren, or to fall themselves by their Hands.

He has excited domestic Insurrections amongst us, and has endeavoured to bring on the Inhabitants of our Frontiers, the merciless Indian Savages, whose known Rule of Warfare, is an undistinguished Destruction, of all Ages, Sexes and Conditions.

In every stage of these Oppressions we have Petitioned for Redress in the most humble Terms: Our repeated Petitions have been answered only by repeated Injury. A Prince, whose

Character is thus marked by every act which may define a Tyrant, is unfit to be the Ruler of a free People.

Nor have we been wanting in Attentions to our British Brethren. We have warned them from Time to Time of Attempts by their Legislature to extend an unwarrantable Jurisdiction over us. We have reminded them of the Circumstances of our Emigration and Settlement here. We have appealed to their native Justice and Magnanimity, and we have conjured them by the Ties of our common Kindred to disavow these Usurpations, which, would inevitably interrupt our Connections and Correspondence. They too have been deaf to the Voice of Justice and Consanguinity. We must, therefore, acquiesce in the Necessity, which denounces our Separation, and hold them, as we hold the rest of Mankind, Enemies in War, in Peace, Friends.

We, therefore, the Representatives of the UNITED STATES OF AMERICA, in GENERAL CONGRESS, Assembled, appealing to the Supreme Judge of the World for the Rectitude of our Intentions, do, in the Name, and by Authority of the good People of these Colonies, solemnly Publish and Declare, That these United Colonies are, and of Right ought to be, FREE AND INDEPENDENT STATES; that they are Absolved from all Allegiance to the British Crown, and that all political Connection between them and the State of Great-Britain, is and ought to be totally dissolved: and that as FREE AND INDE-

PENDENT STATES, they have full Power to levy War, conclude Peace, contract Alliances, establish Commerce, and to do all other Acts and Things which INDEPENDENT STATES may of right do. And for the support of this Declaration, with a firm reliance on the Protection of divine Providence, we mutually pledge to each other our Lives, our Fortunes, and our sacred Honor.

Source: A Declaration By the Representatives of the United States of America, In General Congress Assembled (Philadelphia, 1776).

[Jeremy Bentham,]
Short Review of the Declaration (1776)

In examining this singular Declaration, I have hitherto confined myself to what are given as *facts,* and alleged against his Majesty and his Parliament, in support of the charge of tyranny and usurpation. Of the preamble I have taken little or no notice. The truth is, little or none does it deserve. The opinions of the modern Americans on Government, like those of their good ancestors on witchcraft, would be too ridiculous to deserve any notice, if like them too, contemptible and extravagant as they be, they had not led to the most serious evils.

In this preamble however it is, that they attempt to establish a *theory of Government;* a theory, as absurd and visionary, as the system of conduct in defence of which it is established, is nefarious. Here it is, that maxims are advanced in justification of their enterprises against the British Government. To these maxims, adduced for *this purpose,* it would be sufficient to say, that they are *repugnant to the British Constitution.* But beyond this they are subversive of every actual or imaginable kind of Government.

They are about "*to assume,*" as they tell us, "*among the powers of the earth, that equal and separate station to which*"—they have lately discovered—*"the laws of Nature, and of Nature's God entitle them."* What difference these acute legislators suppose between the laws of *Nature,* and of *Nature's God,* is more than I can take upon me to determine, or even to guess. If to what they now demand they were entitled by any law of God, they had only to produce that law, all controversy was at an end. Instead of this, what do they produce? What they call self-evident truths. *"All men,"* they tell us, "are created equal." This surely is a new discovery; now, for the first time, we learn, that a child, at the moment of his birth, has the same quantity of *natural* power as the parent, the same quantity of *political* power as the magistrate.

The rights of *"life, liberty,* and the *pursuit of happiness"*—by which, if they mean any thing, they must mean the right to *enjoy* life, to *enjoy* liberty, and to *pursue* happiness—they *"hold to be unalienable."* This they "hold to be among *truths self-evident."* At the same time, to secure these rights, they are content that Governments should be instituted. They perceive not, or will not seem to perceive, that nothing which can be called Government ever was, or ever could be, in any instance, exercised, but at the expense of one or other of those rights.—That, consequently, in as many instance as Government is ever exercised, some one or other of these rights, pretended to be unalienable, is actually alienated.

That men who are engaged in the design of subverting a lawful Government, should endeavour by a cloud of words, to throw a veil over their design; that they should endeavour to beat down the criteria between tyranny and lawful government, is not at all surprising. But rather surprising it must certainly appear, that they should advance maxims so incompatible with their own present conduct. If the right of enjoying life be unalienable, whence came their invasion of his Majesty's province of Canada? Whence the unprovoked destruction of so many lives of the inhabitants of that province? If the right of enjoying liberty be unalienable, whence came so many of his Majesty's peaceable subjects among them, without any offence, without so much as a pretended offence, merely for being suspected not to wish well to their enormities, to be held by them in durance? If the right of pursuing happiness be unalienable, how is that so many others of their fellow-citizens are by the same injustice and violence made miserable, their fortunes ruined, their persons banished and driven from their friends and families? Or would they have it believed, that there is in their selves some superior sanctity, some peculiar privilege, by which those things are lawful to them, which are unlawful to all the world besides? Or is it, that among acts of coercion, acts by which life or liberty are taken away, and the pursuit of happiness restrained, those only are unlawful, which their delinquency has brought upon them, and which are exercised by regular, long established, accustomed governments?

In these tenets, they have outdone the utmost extravangance of all former fanatics. The German Anabaptists indeed went so far as to speak of the right of enjoying life as a right unalienable. To take away life, even in the Magistrate, they held to be unlawful. But they went no farther, it was reserved for an American Congress, to add to the number of unalienable rights, that of enjoying liberty, and pursuing happiness;—that is,—if they mean anything,—pursuing it wherever a man thinks he can see it, and by whatever means he thinks he can attain it:—That is, that all *penal* laws—those made by their selves among others— which affect life or liberty, are contrary to the law of God, and the unalienable rights of mankind:—That is, that thieves are not to be restrained from theft, murderers from murder, rebels from rebellion.

Here then they have put the axe to the root of all Government; and yet, in the same breath, they talk of "Governments," of Governments "long established." To these last, they attribute some kind of respect; they vouchsafe even to go so far as to admit, that *"Governments, long established, should not be changed for light or transient reasons."*

Yet they are about to *change* a Government, a Government whose establishment is coeval with their own existence as a Community. What causes do they assign? Circumstances which have always subsisted, which must continue to subsist, wherever Government has subsisted, or can subsist.

For what, according to their own shewing, what was their original, their *only original grievance?* That they were actually taxed more than they could bear? No; but that they were *liable*

to be so taxed. What is the amount of all the *subsequent* grievances they allege? That they were *actually* oppressed by Government? That Government had *actually* misused its power?
No; but that it was *possible* they might be oppressed; *possible* that
Government might misuse its powers. Is there any where, can
there be imagined any where, *that* Government, where subjects
are not liable to be taxed more than they can bear? where is it
not possible that subjects may be oppressed, not possible that
Government may misuse its powers?

This, I say, is the amount, the *whole sum and substance of all*
their grievances. For in taking a general review of the charges
brought against his Majesty, and his Parliament, we may observe that there is a studied confusion in the arrangement of
them. It may therefore be worth while to reduce them to the
several distinct heads, under which I should have classed them
at the first, had not the order of the Answer been necessarily
prescribed by the order—or rather the disorder—of the Declaration.

The first head consists of Acts of *Government,* charged as so
many acts of *incroachment,* so many *usurpations* upon the present
King and his Parliaments exclusively, which had been constantly
exercised by his Predecessors and their Parliaments.

In all the articles comprised in this head, is there a single
power alleged to have been exercised during the present reign,
which had not been constantly exercised by preceding Kings,
and preceding Parliaments? Read only the commission and in-

struction for the Council of Trade, drawn up in the 9th of King William III, addressed to Mr. *Locke,* and others. See there what powers were exercised by the King and Parliament over the Colonies. Certainly the Commissioners were directed to inquire into, and make their reports concerning those matters only, in which the King and Parliament had a power of controlling the Colonies. Now the Commissioners are instructed to inquire—into the condition of the Plantations, "as well with regard to the *administration of Government and Justice,* as in relation to the commerce thereof;"—into the means of making "them *most beneficial and useful to England; into the staples and manufactures, which may be encouraged there;*"—"into the means of *diverting them from such trades.*" Farther, they are instructed "*to examine into, and weigh the Acts of the Assemblies* of the Plantations;"—"*to set down the usefulness or mischief to the Crown, to the Kingdom, or to the Plantations their selves.*"—And farther still, they are instructed "*to require an account of all the monies given for public uses by the Assemblies of the Plantations, and how the same are, or have been expended, or laid out.*" Is there now a single Act of the present reign which does not fall under one or other of these instructions.

The powers then, of which the several articles now before us complain, are supported by usage; were conceived to be supported *then,* just after the Revolution, at the same time these instructions were given; and were they to be supported *only* upon this foot of usage, still that usage being coeval with the Colonies, their tacit consent and approbation, through all the successive periods in which that usage has prevailed, would be implied;—even then the legality of those powers would stand upon the same foot as most of the prerogatives of the Crown, most of the rights of the people;—even then the exercise of those powers could in no wise be deemed usurpations or encroachments.

But the truth is, to the exercise of these powers, the Colonies have not only tacitly, but *expressly,* consented; as expressly as any subject of Great Britain ever consented to the Acts of the British Parliament. Consult the Journals of either House of Parliament; consult the proceedings of their own Assemblies; and innumerable will be the occasions, on which the legality of these powers will be found to be expressly recognised by Acts of the Colonial Assemblies. For in preceding reigns, the petitions from these Assemblies were couched in a language, very different from that which they have assumed under the present reign. In praying for the non-exercise of these powers, in particular instances, they acknowledged their legality; the right in general was recognised; the exercise of it, in particular instances, was prayed to be suspended on the sole ground of *inexpedience.*

The less reason can the Americans have to complain against the exercise of these powers, as it was under the constant exercise of the self-same powers, that they have grown up with a vigour and rapidity unexampled: That within a period, in which other communities have scarcely had time to take root, they have shot forth exuberant branches. So flourishing is their agriculture, that—we are told—"besides feeding plentifully their own growing multitudes, their annual exports have exceeded a *million:*" So flourishing is their trade, that—we are told—"it has increased far beyond the speculations of the most sanguine imagination." So powerful are they in arms, that we see them defy the united force of that nation, which, but a little century ago, called them into being; which, but a few years ago, in their defence, encountered and subdued almost the united force of Europe.

If the exercise of powers, thus established by usage, thus recognised by express declarations, thus sanctified by their beneficial effects, can justify rebellion, there is not that subject in the world, but who has, ever has had, and ever must have, reason sufficient to rebel: There never was, never can be, established, any government upon earth.

The second head consists of Acts, whose professed object was either the maintenance, or the amendment of their Constitution. These Acts were passed with the view either of freeing from impediments the course of their *commercial* transactions, or of facilitating the administration of justice, or of poising more equally the different powers in their Constitution; or of preventing the establishment of Courts, inconsistent with the spirit of the Constitution.

To state the object of these Acts, is to justify them. Acts of *tyranny* they cannot be: Acts of *usurpation* they *are not;* because no new power is assumed. By former Parliaments, in former reigns, officers of *customs* had been sent to America: Courts of Admiralty had been established there. The increase of trade and population induced the Parliaments, under the present reign, for the *convenience* of the Colonists, and to obviate *their own objections* of delays arising from appeals to England, to establish a Board of Customs, and an Admiralty Court of Appeal. Strange indeed is it to hear the establishment of this Board, and these Courts, alleged as proofs of *usurpation;* and in the same paper, in the same breath, to hear it urged as a head of *complaint,* that his Majesty refused his assent to a much greater exertion of power:—to an exertion of power, which might be dangerous; the establishment of new Courts of Judicature. What in one instance he might have done, to have done in another, cannot be unconstitutional. In former reigns, charters have been altered; in the present reign, the constitution of one charter, having been found inconsistent with the ends of good order and government, was amended.

The third head consists of temporary Acts, passed *pro re natâ,* the object of each of which was to remedy some temporary evil, and the duration of which was restrained to the duration of the evil itself.

Neither in these Acts was any new power assumed; in some instances only, the objects upon which that power was exercised, were new. Nothing was done but what former Kings and former Parliaments have shewn their selves ready to do, had the same circumstances subsisted. The same circumstances never did subsist before, because, till the present reign, the Colonies never dared to call in question the supreme authority of Parliament.

No charge, classed under this head, can be called a *grievance*. Then only is the subject aggrieved, when, paying *due obedience* to the established Laws of his country, he is not protected in his established rights. From the moment he withholds *obedience,* he forfeits his right to *protection*. Nor can the means, employed to bring him back to obedience, however severe, be called griev-ances; especially if those means be to cease the very moment that the end is obtained.

The last head consists of Acts of self-defence, exercised in *consequence* of resistance already shewn, but represented in the Declaration as Acts of oppression, tending to provoke resis-tance. Has his Majesty cut off their trade with all parts of the world? They first attempted to cut off the trade of Great Brit-ain. Has his Majesty ordered their vessels to be seized? They first burnt the vessels of the King. Has his Majesty sent troops to chastise them? They first took up arms against the authority of the King. Has his Majesty engaged the Indians against them? They first engaged Indians against the troops of the King. Has his Majesty commanded their captives to serve on board his fleet? He has only saved them from the gallows.

By some, these acts have been improperly called *"Acts of punishment."* And we are then asked, with an air of insult, "What! will you punish without a trial, without a hearing?" And no doubt punishment, whether ordinary or extraordinary; whether by *indictment, impeachment,* or bill of *attainder,* should be preceded by judicial examination. But, the acts comprised under this head are not acts of punishment; they are, as we have called them, acts of *self-defence.* And these are not, cannot be, preceded by any judicial examination. An example or two will serve to place the difference between acts of punishment and acts of self-defence in a stronger light, than any definition we can give. It has happened, that bodies of manufacturers have risen, and armed, in order to compel their masters to increase their wages: It has happened, that bodies of peasants have risen, and armed, in order to compel the farmer to sell at a lower price. It has happened, that the civil magistrate, unable to reduce the insurgents to their duty, has called the military to his aid. But did ever any man imagine, that the military were sent to punish the insurgents? It has happened, that the insurgents have resisted the military, as they had resisted the civil magistrate: It has happened, that, in consequence of this resistance, some of the insurgents have been killed:—But did ever any man imagine that those who were then killed, were therefore *punished?* No more can they be said to be punished, than could the incendiary, who should be buried beneath the ruins of the house, which he had feloniously set on fire. Take an example yet nearer to the present case. When the Duke of Cumberland led the armies of the king, *foreign and domestic,* against the Rebels in Scotland, did any man conceive that he was sent to *punish* the Rebels?—Clearly not.—He was sent to protect dutiful and loyal subjects, who remained in the peace of the King, against the outrages of Rebels, who had broken the peace of the King.—Does any man speak of those who fell at the battle of Culloden, as of men that were *punished?* Would that man have been thought in his senses, who should have urged, that the armies of the King should not have ben sent against the Rebels in Scotland, till those very Rebels had been judicially heard, and judicially convicted? Does not every man feel the fact, the *only* fact, necessary to be known, in order to justify these acts of self-defence, is simply this:—Are men in arms against the authority of the King?—Who does not feel, that to authenticate this fact, demands no judicial inquiry? If when his Royal Highness had led the army under his command into Scotland, there had been no body of men in arms; if, terrified at his approach, they had either laid down their arms and submitted, or had dispersed and retired quietly, each to his own home, what would have been the consequence? The civil magistrate would have searched for and seized upon those who *had* been in arms; would have brought them to a court of justice: That court would have proceeded to examine, and to condemn or to acquit, as evidence was, or was not, given of the guilt of the respective culprits. The Rebels did not submit, they did not lay down their arms, they did not disperse; they resisted the Duke: a battle ensued: some of the Rebels fled, others were slain, others taken. It is upon those only of the *last* class, who were brought before and condemned by Courts of Justice, that *punishment* was inflicted. By what kind of logic then are these acts ranked in the class of grievances?

These are the Acts—these exertions of constitutional, and hitherto, *undisputed* powers, for which, in this audacious paper, a patriot King is traduced—as "a Prince, whose character is marked by every Act which may define a tyrant;" as "unfit to be the ruler of a free people." These are the Acts, these exertions of constitutional, and, hitherto, undisputed powers, by which the Members of the Congress declare their selves and their constituents to be "absolved from all allegiance to the British Crown;" pronounce "all political connection between Great Britain and America to be totally dissolved." With that hypocrisy which pervades the whole of the Declaration, they pretend indeed, that this event is not of their seeking; that it is forced upon them; that they only *"acquiesce in the necessity which denounces their separation from us:"* which compels them hereafter to hold us, as they "hold the rest of mankind; *enemies in war; in peace, friends."*

How this Declaration may strike others, I know not. To me, I own, it appears that it cannot fail—to use the words of a great

Orator—"of doing us *Knight*'s service." The mouth of faction, we may reasonably presume, will be closed; the eyes of those who saw not, or would not see, that the Americans were long since aspiring at independence, will be opened; the nation will unite as one man, and teach this rebellious people, that it is one thing for them to *say,* the connection, which bound them to us, is *dissolved,* another to *dissolve* it; that to *accomplish* their *independence* is not quite so easy as to *declare* it: *that there is no peace with them, but with the peace of the King: no war with them, but that war, which offended justice wages against criminals.*—We too, I hope, shall *acquiesce in the necessity* of submitting to whatever burdens, of making whatever efforts may be necessary, to bring this ungrateful and rebellious people back to that allegiance they have long had it in contemplation to renounce, and have now at last so daringly renounced.

Source: [John Lind and Jeremy Bentham,] *An Answer to the Declaration of the American Congress* (London, 1776), 119–132.

Manifesto of the Province of Flanders [extracts]
(January 4, 1790)

Greetings from the Estates of Flanders to those who will read or hear these words.

Since it has pleased Divine Providence to restore our natural rights of liberty and independence by severing the bonds that once fastened us to a Prince and a House whose domination was ever harmful to the interests of Flanders, we feel obliged to recount for present and future generations the events which inspired and accomplished this happy Revolution.

Flanders enjoyed natural and uninterrupted prosperity due to a fertile soil, a fortunate location, and the innate industriousness of its people so long as its sovereigns ruled while residing in the country. The old Counts of Flanders and later the Princes of the House of Burgundy were born and raised among their subjects and thus held the same principles in common. They were guided by the national interest and they molded their conduct to the spirit of the People. They respected those traditional rights, privileges, freedoms and exemptions that are no different, in their essentials, to the natural rights of man and citizen.

They understood the inviolable character of the bond between them and the Nation as established by oath during the solemn act of inauguration. If there were disagreements between the Sovereign and his subjects, the fact of his immediate presence made it possible to reach a swift compromise and to avert dangerous repercussions. With the support of a mild and just government, Flanders attained the heights of greatness with little apparent effort. The towns of Ghent and Bruges were unsurpassed in their splendor and riches. The whole of Flanders gave the impression of a single and unified City. The Court of its Count, Philip of Burgundy, was assuredly the most brilliant in Europe.

That same Prince founded the Order of the Golden Fleece in the town of Bruges, which remains famous throughout Europe today. Flanders and Belgium became the center of the arts and sciences in years that Austria, which now affects to educate us, was still plunged in barbarism.

This prosperity continued to increase until the marriage of the Archduke Maximilian with the Princess Marie of Burgundy, when Flanders passed to the House of Austria.

That marriage marked the apogee of Flemish greatness and the beginning of its decline. When Flanders became one among many states ruled by the House of Austria, it became a state of secondary importance that could even seem foreign to its own sovereigns, through its remoteness from the primary Austrian lands, where the Princes made their abode. . . .

. . . it is incontestable that the Emperor has broken all of his agreements with us. By violating the social and inaugural pact, he freed the Nation to sever its bond of obedience. Moreover, he has remained deaf to the humble and renewed appeals of a Nation that sought redress for its grievances until the final hour. In waging war upon us, the Emperor obliged us to meet force with force and to claim all those rights granted by the Law of Nations to victorious parties. If it is true that the Emperor, in conquering us, could have claimed the right to treat us as a conquered People, as the Minister suggests in his Manifesto of 20 November [1789], the Law of Nations and the natural law of reciprocity permits that we who have been favored by success should defy his claim to our obedience and enter a state of complete liberty and independence.

In consequence, in accordance with our preceding resolutions and declarations, before the Supreme Judge of the World who knows the justice of our cause, we solemnly publish and declare in the name of the People that this Province is and of right ought to be a Free and Independent State; that it has been absolved from all allegiance to the Emperor Joseph II, Count of Flanders, and to the House of Austria. We further declare that the individual members of all orders civil and military are absolved and disengaged from any obedience and fidelity to the said Emperor. We further declare that all officials, justices, vassals and vavasours, of whatever quality or rank, are liberated from all agreements and freed of all obligations pledged or owed to the Emperor in his capacity as the Count of Flanders.

We forbid all officers, justices, employees and others to employ or make use of the titles or arms of the former Count of Flanders. We command them to use the seal and the arms of this Province until they receive further instructions. All official acts, dispatches and letters of any kind shall be deemed null if passed, signed or sealed otherwise.

In order to implement these instructions, we order that the seals and arms of the Emperor Joseph II, former Count of Flanders, be remitted immediately into the hands of the Estates.

In addition, we declare and command that no coin be struck hereafter with the arms of the former Count. Until further arrangements are made, the money in use in this province will remain legal tender.

We declare the Jurisdiction of the Great Council over this country and the inhabitants of this Province to be hereafter null.

We demand that the present declaration be printed, publicized, and posted in the Province of Flanders in the usual places and wherever there is need, so that no person can claim ignorance of its contents.

We order members of the Council of Flanders, which the present document erects as Sovereign Council of Justice, to observe punctually and cause to be observed the entire content of these instructions. Signed and sealed in our Assembly, 4 January 1790.

Source: J. F. Rohaert, *Manifeste de la Province de Flandre* (Ghent, 1790), 3–5, 22–24 (translated).

The Haitian Declaration of Independence
(January 1, 1804)

The General in Chief to the People of Hayti,

Citizens,

It is not enough to have expelled from your country the barbarians who have for ages stained it with blood—it is not enough to have curbed the factions which, succeeding each other by turns, sported with a phantom of liberty which France exposed to their eyes. It is become necessary, by a last act of national authority, to ensure for ever the empire of liberty in the country which has given us birth. It is necessary to deprive an inhuman government, which has hitherto held our minds in a state of the most humiliating torpitude, of every hope of being enabled again to enslave us. Finally, it is necessary to live independent, or die. Independence or Death! Let these sacred words serve to rally us—let them be signals of battle, and of our re-union.

Citizens—Countrymen—I have assembled on this solemn day, those courageous chiefs, who, on the eve of receiving the last breath of expiring liberty, have lavished their blood to preserve it. These generals, who have conducted your struggles against tyranny, have not yet done. The French name still darkens our plains: every thing recalls the remembrance of the cruelties of that barbarous people. Our laws, our customs, our cities, every thing bears the characteristic of the French,—Hearken to what I say!—the French still have a footing in our island! and you believe yourselves free and independent of that republic, which has fought all nations, it is true, but never conquered those who would be free! What! victims for fourteen years by credulity and forbearance! conquered not by French armies, but by the canting eloquence of the proclamations of their agents! When shall we be wearied with breathing the same air with them? What have we in common with that bloody-minded people? Their cruelties compared to our moderation—their colour to ours—the extension of seas which separate us—our avenging climate—all plainly tell us they are not our brethren; that they never will become such; and, if they find an asylum among us, they will still be the instigators of our troubles and of our divisions. Citizens, men, women, young and old, cast round your eyes on every part of this island; seek there your wives, your husbands, your brothers, your sisters—what did I say? seek your children—your children at the breast, what is become of them? I shudder to tell it—the *prey of vultures.* Instead of these interesting victims, the affrighted eye sees only their assassins—tigers still covered with their blood, and whose terrifying presence reproaches you for your insensibility, and your guilty tardiness to avenge them—what do you wait for, to appease their manes? Remember that you have wished your remains to be laid by the side of your fathers—When you have driven out tyranny—will you descend into their tombs, without having avenged them? No: their bones would repulse yours. And ye, invaluable men, intrepid Generals, who insensible to private sufferings, have given new life to liberty, by lavishing your blood; know, that you have done nothing if you do not give to the nations a terrible, though just example, of the vengeance that ought to be exercised by a people proud of having recovered its liberty, and zealous of maintaining it. Let us intimidate those, who might dare to attempt depriving us of it again: let us begin with the French; let them shudder at approaching our shores, if not on account of the cruelties they have committed, at least at the terrible resolution we are going to make—To devote to death whatsoever native of France should soil with his sacrilegious footstep, this territory of liberty.

We have dared to be free—let us continue free by ourselves, and for ourselves; let us imitate the growing child; his own strength breaks his leading-strings, which become useless and troublesome to him in his walk. What are the people who have fought us? what people would reap the fruits of our labours? and what dishonourable absurdity, to conquer to be slaves!

Slaves—leave to the French nation this odious epithet; they have conquered to be no longer free—let us walk in other footsteps; let us imitate other nations, who, carrying their solicitude into futurity, and dreading to leave posterity an example of cowardice, have preferred to be exterminated, rather than be erased from the list of free people. Let us, at the same time, take care, lest a spirit of proselytism should destroy the work—let our neighbours breathe in peace—let them live peaceably under the shield of those laws which they have framed for themselves; let us beware of becoming revolutionary fire-brands—of creating ourselves the legislators of the Antilles—of considering as a glory the disturbing the tranquility of the neighboring islands; they have not been, like the one we inhabit, drenched with the innocent blood of the inhabitants— they have no vengeance to exercise against the authority that protects them; happy, never to have experienced the pestilence that has destroyed us, they must wish well to our posterity.

Peace with our neighbours, but accursed be the French name—eternal hatred to France: such are our principles.

Natives of Hayti—my happy destiny reserves me to be one day the centinel who is to guard the idol we now sacrifice to. I have grown old fighting for you, sometimes almost alone; and if I have been happy enough to deliver to you the sacred charge confided to me, recollect it is for you, at present, to preserve it. In fighting for your liberty, I have laboured for my own happiness: before it shall be consolidated by laws which shall ensure individual liberty, your chiefs whom I have assembled here, and myself, owe you this last proof of our devotedness.

Generals, and other chiefs, unite with me for the happiness of our country: the day is arrived—the day which will ever perpetuate our glory and our independence.

If there exist among you a lukewarm heart, let him retire, and shudder to pronounce the oath which is to unite us. Let us swear to the whole world, to posterity, to ourselves, to renounce France for ever, and to die, rather than live under its dominion—to fight till the last breath for the independence of our country.

And ye, people, too long unfortunate, witness the oath we now pronounce: recollect that it is upon your constancy and courage I depended when I first entered the career of liberty to fight despotism and tyranny, against which you have been struggling these last fourteen years; remember that I have sacrificed every thing to fly to your defence—parents, children, fortune, and am now only rich, in your liberty—that my name has become a horror to all friends of slavery, or despots; and tyrants only pronounce it, cursing the day that gave me birth; if ever you refuse or receive with murmuring the laws, which the protecting angel that watches over your destinies, shall dictate to me for your happiness, you will merit the fate of an ungrateful people. But away from me this frightful idea: You will be the guardians of the liberty you cherish, the support of the Chief who commands you.

Swear then to live free and independent, and to prefer death to every thing that would lead to replace you under the yoke; swear then to pursue for everlasting, the traitors, and enemies of your independence.

J. J. DESSALINES.

Head-quarters, Gonaïves,

1st Jan. 1804, 1st Year of Independence.

Source: Marcus Rainsford, *An Historical Account of the Black Empire of Hayti: Comprehending a View of the Principal Transactions in the Revolution of Saint-Domingo; with its Ancient and Modern State* (London, 1805), 442–446.

The Venezuelan Declaration of Independence
(July 5, 1811)

In the Name of the All-powerful God,

We, the Representatives of the united Provinces of Caracas, Cumana, Varinas, Margarita, Barcelona, Merida, and Truxillo, forming the American Confederation of Venezuela, in the South Continent, in Congress assembled, considering the full and absolute possession of our Rights, which we recovered justly and legally from the 19th of April, 1810, in consequence of the occurrences in Bayona, and the occupation of the Spanish Throne by conquest, and the succession of a new Dynasty, constituted without our consent: are desirous, before we make use of those Rights, of which we have been deprived by force for more than three ages, but now restored to us by the political order of human events, to make known to the world the reasons which have emanated from these same occurrences, and which authorise us in the free use we are now about to make of our own Sovereignty.

We do not wish, nevertheless, to begin by alledging the rights inherent in every conquered country, to recover its state of property and independence; we generously forget the long series of ills, injuries, and privations, which the sad right of conquest has indistinctly caused, to all the descendants of the Discoverers, Conquerors, and Settlers of these Countries, plunged into a worse state by the very same cause that ought to have favoured them; and drawing a veil over the 300 years of Spanish dominion in America, we will now only present the authentic and well-known facts, which ought to have wrested from one world, the right over the other, by the inversion, disorder, and conquest, that have already dissolved the Spanish Nation.

This disorder has increased the ills of America, by rendering void its claims and remonstrances, enabling the Governors of Spain to insult and oppress us this part of the Nation, thus leaving it without the succour and guarantee of the Laws.

It is contrary to order, impossible to the Government of Spain, and fatal to the welfare of America, that the latter, possessed of a range of country infinitely more extensive, and a population incomparably more numerous, should depend and be subject to a Peninsular Corner of the European Continent.

The Cessions and Abdications made at Bayona, the Revolutions of the Escurial and Aranjuez, and the Orders of the Royal Substitute, the Duke of Berg, sent to America, suffice to give virtue to the rights, which till then the Americans had sacrificed to the unity and integrity of the Spanish Nation.

Venezuela was the first to acknowledge, and generously to preserve, this integrity; not to abandon the cause of its brothers, as long as the same retained the least hope of salvation.

America was called into a new existence, since she could, and ought, to take upon herself the charge of her own fate and preservation; as Spain might acknowledge, or not, the rights of a King, who had preferred his own existence to the dignity of the Nation over which he governed.

All the Bourbons concurred to the invalid stipulations of Bayona, abandoning the country of Spain, against the will of the People;—they violated, disdained, and trampled on the sacred duty they had contracted with the Spaniards of both Worlds, when with their blood and treasure they had placed them on the Throne, in despite of the House of Austria. By such a conduct, they were left disqualified and incapable of governing a Free People, whom they have delivered up like a flock of Slaves.

The intrusive Governments that arrogated to themselves the National Representation, took advantage of the dispositions which the good faith, distance, oppression, and ignorance, created in the Americans, against the new Dynasty that had entered Spain by means of force; and, contrary to their own principles, they sustained amongst us the illusion in favour of Ferdinand, in order to devour and harass us with impunity: at most, they promised to us liberty, equality, and fraternity, conveyed in pompous discourses and studied phrases, for the purpose of covering the snare laid by a cunning, useless, and degrading Representation.

As soon as they were dissolved, and had substituted and destroyed amongst themselves the various forms of the Government of Spain; and as soon as the imperious law of necessity had dictated to Venezuela the urgency of preserving itself, in order to guard and maintain the rights of her King, and to offer an asylum to her European brethren against the ills that threatened them; their former conduct was divulged: they varied their principles, and gave their appellations of insurrection, perfidy, and ingratitude, to the same acts that had served as models for the Governments of Spain; because then was closed to them the gate to the monopoly of administration, which they meant to perpetuate, under the name of an imaginary King.

Notwithstanding our protests, our moderation, generosity, and the inviolability of our principles, contrary to the wishes of our brethren in Europe, we were declared in a state of rebellion; we were blockaded; war was declared against us; agents were sent amongst us, to excite us one against the other, endeavouring to take away our credit with the other Nations of Europe, by imploring their assistance to oppress us.

Without taking the least notice of our reasons, without presenting them to the impartial judgment of the world, and without any other judges than our own enemies, we are condemned to a mournful incommunication with our brethren; and, to add contempt to calumny, empowered agents are named for us against our own express will, that in their Cortes they may arbitrarily dispose of our interests, under the influence and force of our enemies.

In order to crush and suppress the effects of our Representation, when they were obliged to grant it to us, we were submitted to a paltry and diminutive scale; and the form of election was subjected to the passive voice of the Municipal Bodies, degraded by the despotism of the Governors: which amounted to an insult to our plain dealing and good faith, more than a consideration of our incontestable political importance.

Always deaf to the cries of justice on our part, the Governments of Spain have endeavoured to discredit all our efforts, by declaring us criminal, and stamping with infamy, and rewarding with the scaffold and confiscation, every attempt, which at different periods some Americans have made, for the felicity of their country: as was that which lately our own security dictated to us, that we might not be driven into a state of disorder which we foresaw, and hurried to that horrid fate which we are about to remove for ever from before us. By means of such atrocious policy, they have succeeded in making our brethren insensible to our misfortunes; in arming them against us; in erasing from their bosoms the sweet impressions of friendship, of consanguinity; and converting into enemies a part of our own great family.

At a time that we, faithful to our promises, were sacrificing our security and civil dignity, not to abandon the rights which we have generously preserved to Ferdinand of Bourbon, we have seen that, to the relations of force which bound him to the Emperor of the French, he has added the ties of blood and friendship; in consequence of which, even the Governments of Spain have already declared their resolution only to acknowledge him conditionally.

In this mournful alternative we have remained three years, in a state of political indecision and ambiguity, so fatal and dangerous, that this alone would suffice to authorise the resolution, which the faith of our promises and the bonds of fraternity had caused us to defer, till necessity has obliged us to go beyond what we at first proposed, impelled by the hostile and unnatural conduct of the Governments of Spain, which have disburdened us of our conditional oath, by which circumstance, we are called to the august representation we now exercise.

But we, who glory in grounding our proceedings on better principles, and not wishing to establish our felicity on the misfortunes of our fellow-beings, do consider and declare as friends, companions of our fate, and participators of our felicity those who, united to us by the ties of blood, language, and religion, have suffered the same evils in the anterior order of things, provided they acknowledge our *absolute independence* of the same, and of any other foreign power whatever; and that they aid us to sustain it with their lives, fortune, and sentiments; declaring and acknowledging them (as well as to every other nation,) in war enemies, and in peace friends, brothers, and co-patriots.

In consequence of all these solid, public, and incontestible reasons of policy, which so powerfully urge the necessity of recovering our natural dignity, restored to us by the order of events; and in compliance with the imprescriptible rights enjoyed by nations, to destroy every pact, agreement, or association, which does not answer the purposes for which governments were established; we believe that we cannot, nor ought not, to preserve the bonds which hitherto kept us united to the Government of Spain: and that, like all the other nations of the world, we are free, and authorised not to depend on any other authority than our own, and to take amongst the powers of the earth the place of equality which the Supreme Being and Nature assign to us, and to which we are called by the succession of human events, and urged by our own good and utility.

Notwithstanding we are aware of the difficulties that attend, and the obligations imposed upon us, by the rank we are about to take in the political order of the world; as well as the powerful influence of forms and habitudes, to which unfortunately we have been accustomed: we at the same time know, that the shameful submission to them, when we can throw them off, would be still more ignominious for us, and more fatal to our posterity, than our long and painful slavery; and that it now becomes an indispensable duty to provide for our preservation, security, and felicity, by essentially varying all the forms of our former constitution.

In consequence whereof, considering, by the reasons thus

alledged, that we have satisfied the respect which we owe to the opinions of the human race, and the dignity of other nations, in the number of whom we are about to enter, and on whose communication and friendship we rely: We, the Representatives of the United Provinces of Venezuela, calling on the SUPREME BEING to witness the justice of our proceedings and the rectitude of our intentions, do implore his divine and celestial help; and ratifying, at the moment in which we are born to the dignity to which his Providence restores to us, the desire we have of living and dying free, and of believing and defending the holy Catholic and Apostolic Religion of Jesus Christ. We, therefore, in the name and by the will and authority which we hold from the virtuous People of Venezuela, DO declare solemnly to the world, that its united Provinces are, and ought to be, from this day, by act and right, Free, Sovereign and Independent States; and that they are absolved from every submission and dependence on the Throne of Spain, or on those who do, or may call themselves, its Agents and Representatives; and that a free and independent State, thus constituted, has full power to take that form of Government which may be conformable to the general will of the People, to declare war, make peace, form alliances, regulate treaties of commerce, limits, and navigation; and to do and transact every act, in like manner as other free and independent States. And that this, our solemn Declaration, may be held valid, firm, and durable, we hereby pledge our lives, fortunes, and the sacred tie of our national honour. Done in the Federal Palace of Caracas; signed by our own hands, sealed with the great Provisional Seal of the Confederation, and countersigned by the Secretary to the Congress, on the 5th day of July, 1811, the first of our Independence.

Source: Interesting Official Documents Relating to The United Provinces of Venezuela (London, 1812), 3–19.

Declaration of the Independence of New Zealand
(October 28, 1835)

1. We, the hereditary chiefs and heads of the tribes of the Northern parts of New Zealand, being assembled at Waitangi in the Bay of Islands on this 28th day of October, 1835, declare the Independence of our Country, which is hereby constituted and declared to be an Independent State, under the designation of The United Tribes of New Zealand.

2. All sovereign power and authority within the territories of the United Tribes of New Zealand is hereby declared to reside entirely and exclusively in the hereditary chiefs and heads of tribes in their collective capacity, who also declare that they will not permit any legislative authority separate from themselves in their collective capacity to exist, nor any function of government to be exercised within the said territories, unless by persons appointed by them, and acting under the authority of laws regularly enacted by them in Congress assembled.

3. The hereditary chiefs and heads of tribes agree to meet in Congress at Waitangi in the autumn of each year, for the purpose of framing laws for the dispensation of justice, the preservation of peace and good order, and the regulation of trade; and they cordially invite the Southern tribes to lay aside their pri-

vate animosities and to consult the safety and welfare of our common country, by joining the Confederation of the United Tribes.

4. They also agree to send a copy of this Declaration to His Majesty the King of England, to thank him for his acknowledgement of their flag; and in return for the friendship and protection they have shown, and are prepared to show, to such of his subjects as have settled in their country, or resorted to its shores for the purposes of trade, they entreat that he will continue to be the parent of their infant State, and that he will become its Protector from all attempts upon its independence.

Agreed to unanimously on this 28th day of October, 1835, in the presence of His Britannic Majesty's Resident.

Source: Fac-Similes of the Declaration of Independence and the Treaty of Waitangi (Wellington, NZ, 1877), 4.

The Unanimous Declaration of Independence made by the Delegates of the People of Texas (March 2, 1836)

When a government has ceased to protect the lives, liberty and property of the people, from whom its legitimate powers are derived, and for the advancement of whose happiness it was instituted; and so far from being a guarantee for their inestimable and inalienable rights, becomes an instrument in the hands of evil rulers for their oppression. When the federal republican constitution of their country, which they have sworn to support, no longer has a substantial existence, and the whole nature of their government has been forcibly changed, without their consent, from a restricted federative republic, composed of sovereign states, to a consolidated central military despotism, in which every interest is disregarded but that of the army and the priesthood, both the eternal enemies of civil liberty, the ever ready minions of power, and the usual instruments of tyrants. When, long after the spirit of the constitution has departed, moderation is at length so far lost by those in power, that even the semblance of freedom is removed, and the forms themselves of the constitution discontinued, and so far from their petitions and remonstrances being regarded, the agents who bear them are thrown into dungeons, and mercenary armies sent forth to enforce a new government upon them at the point of the bayonet.

When, in consequence of such acts of malfeasance and abduction on the part of the government, anarchy prevails, and civil society is dissolved into its original elements, in such a crisis, the first law of nature, the right of self-preservation, the inherent and inalienable right of the people to appeal to first principles, and take their political affairs into their own hands in extreme cases, enjoins it as a right towards themselves, and a sacred obligation to their posterity, to abolish such government, and create another in its stead, calculated to rescue them from impending dangers, and to secure their welfare and happiness.

Nations, as well as individuals, are amenable for their acts to the public opinion of mankind. A statement of a part of our grievances is therefore submitted to an impartial world, in justification of the hazardous but unavoidable step now taken, of severing our political connection with the Mexican people, and assuming an independent attitude among the nations of the earth.

The Mexican government, by its colonization laws, invited and induced the Anglo American population of Texas to colonize its wilderness under the pledged faith of a written constitution, that they should continue to enjoy that constitutional liberty and republican government to which they had been habituated in the land of their birth, the United States of America.

In this expectation they have been cruelly disappointed, inasmuch as the Mexican nation has acquiesced in the late changes made in the government by General Antonio Lopez de Santa Anna, who, having overturned the constitution of his country, now offers us the cruel alternative, either to abandon our homes, acquired by so many privations, or submit to the most intolerable of all tyranny, the combined despotism of the sword and the priesthood.

It hath sacrificed our welfare to the state of Coahuila, by which our interests have been continually depressed through a jealous and partial course of legislation, carried on at a far distant seat of government, by a hostile majority, in an unknown tongue, and this too, notwithstanding we have petitioned in the humblest terms for the establishment of a separate state government, and have, in accordance with the provisions of the national constitution, presented to the general congress a republican constitution, which was, without a just cause, contemptuously rejected.

It incarcerated in a dungeon, for a long time, one of our citizens, for no other cause but a zealous endeavour to procure the acceptance of our constitution, and the establishment of a state government.

It has failed and refused to secure, on a firm basis, the right of trial by jury, that palladium of civil liberty, and only safe guarantee for the life, liberty, and property of the citizen.

It has failed to establish any public system of education, although possessed of almost boundless resources, (the public domain,) and although it is an axiom in political science, that unless a people are educated and enlightened, it is idle to expect the continuance of civil liberty, or the capacity for self government.

It has suffered the military commandants, stationed among us, to exercise arbitrary acts of oppression and tyranny, thus trampling upon the most sacred rights of the citizen, and rendering the military superior to the civil power.

It has dissolved, by force of arms, the state congress of Coahuila and Texas, and obliged our representatives to fly for their lives from the seat of government, thus depriving us of the fundamental political right of representation.

It has demanded the surrender of a number of our citizens, and ordered military detachments to seize and carry them into the interior for trial, in contempt of the civil authorities, and in defiance of the laws and the constitution.

It has made piratical attacks upon our commerce, by commissioning foreign desperadoes, and authorizing them to seize our vessels, and convey the property of our citizens to far distant ports for confiscation.

It denies us the right of worshipping the Almighty according to the dictates of our own conscience, by the support of a national religion, calculated to promote the temporal interest of its human functionaries, rather than the glory of the true and living God.

It has demanded us to deliver up our arms, which are essential to our defence—the rightful property of freemen—and formidable only to tyrannical governments.

It has invaded our country both by sea and by land, with intent to lay waste our territory, and drive us from our homes; and has now a large mercenary army advancing, to carry on against us a war of extermination.

It has, through its emissaries, incited the merciless savage, with the tomahawk and scalping knife, to massacre the inhabitants of our defenceless frontiers.

It hath been, during the whole time of our connection with it, the contemptible sport and victim of successive military revolutions, and hath continually exhibited every characteristic of a weak, corrupt, and tyrannical government.

These, and other grievances, were patiently borne by the people of Texas until they reached that point at which forbearance ceases to be a virtue. We then took up arms in defence of the national constitution. We appealed to our Mexican brethren for assistance: our appeal has been made in vain; though months have elapsed, no sympathetic response has yet been heard from the interior. We are, therefore, forced to the melancholy conclusion, that the Mexican people have acquiesced in the destruction of their liberty, and the substitution therefor of a military government; that they are unfit to be free, and incapable of self government.

The necessity of self-preservation, therefore, now decrees our eternal political separation.

We, therefore, the delegates, with plenary powers, of the people of Texas, in solemn convention assembled, appealing to a candid world for the necessities of our condition, do hereby resolve and declare, that our political connection with the Mexican nation has forever ended, and that the people of Texas do now constitute a free, sovereign, and independent republic, and are fully invested with all the rights and attributes which properly belong to independent nations; and, conscious of the rectitude of our intentions, we fearlessly and confidently commit the issue to the decision of the supreme Arbiter of the destinies of nations.

Source: The Papers of the Texas Revolution, 1835–1836, gen. ed. John H. Jenkins, 10 vols. (Austin, 1973), IV, 493–496.

A Declaration of Independence by the Representatives of the People of the Commonwealth of Liberia (July 16, 1847)

We the representatives of the people of the Commonwealth of Liberia, in Convention assembled, invested with authority for forming a new government, relying upon the aid and protection of the Great Arbiter of human events, do hereby, in the name, and on the behalf of the people of this Commonwealth, publish and declare the said commonwealth a FREE, SOVEREIGN, AND INDEPENDENT STATE, by the name and title of the REPUBLIC OF LIBERIA.

While announcing to the nations of the world the new position which the people of this Republic have felt themselves called upon to assume, courtesy to their opinion seems to demand a brief accompanying statement of the causes which induced them, first to expatriate themselves from the land of their nativity and to form settlements on this barbarous coast, and now to organize their government by the assumption of a sovereign and independent character. Therefore we respectfully ask their attention to the following facts.

We recognise in all men, certain natural and inalienable rights: among these are life, liberty, and the right to acquire, possess, enjoy and defend property. By the practice and consent of men in all ages, some system or form of government is proven to be necessary to exercise, enjoy and secure those rights; and every people have a right to institute a government, and to choose and adopt that system or form of it, which in their opinion will most effectively accomplish these objects, and secure their happiness, which does not interfere with the just rights of others. The right therefore to institute government, and to all the powers necessary to conduct it is an inalienable right, and cannot be resisted without the grossest injustice.

We the people of the Republic of Liberia were originally the inhabitants of the United States of North America.

In some parts of that country, we were debarred by law from all rights and privileges of men—in other parts, public sentiment, more powerful than law, frowned us down.

We were every where shut out from all civil office.

We were excluded from all participation in the government.

We were taxed without our consent.

We were compelled to contribute to the resources of a country, which gave us no protection.

We were made a separate and distinct class, and against us every avenue to improvement was effectually closed. Strangers from all lands of a color different from ours, were preferred before us.

We uttered our complaints, but they were unattended to, or only met by alledging the peculiar institutions of the country.

All hope of a favorable change in our country was thus wholly extinguished in our bosoms, and we looked with anxiety abroad for some asylum from the deep degradation.

The Western coast of Africa was the place selected by American benevolence and philanthropy, for our future home. Removed beyond those influences which depressed us in our native land, it was hoped we would be enabled to enjoy those rights and privileges, and exercise and improve those faculties, which the God of nature has given us in common with the rest of mankind.

Under the auspices of the American Colonization Society, we established ourselves here, on land acquired by purchase from the Lords of the soil.

In an original compact with this Society, we, for important reasons delegated to it certain political powers; while this institution stipulated that whenever the people should become capable of conducting the government, or whenever the people should desire it, this institution would resign the delegated power, peacefully withdraw its supervision, and leave the people to the government of themselves.

Under the auspices and guidance of this institution, which has nobly and in perfect faith redeemed its pledges to the people, we have grown and prospered.

From time to time, our number has been increased by migration from America, and by accessions from native tribes; and from time to time, as circumstances required it, we have extended our borders by the acquisition of land by honorable purchase from the natives of the country.

As our territory has extended, and our population increased our commerce has also increased. The flags of most of the civilized nations of the earth float in our harbors, and their merchants are opening an honorable and profitable trade. Until recently, these visits have been of a uniformly harmonious character, but as they have become more frequent, and to more numerous points of our extending coast, questions have arisen, which it is supposed can be adjusted only by agreement between sovereign powers.

For years past, the American Colonization Society has virtually withdrawn from all direct and active part in the administration of the government, except in the appointment of the Governor, who is also a colonist, for the apparent purpose of testing the ability of the people to conduct the affairs of government, and no complaint of crude legislation, nor of mismanagement, nor of mal-administration has yet been heard.

In view of these facts, this institution, the American Colonization Society, with that good faith which has uniformly marked all its dealings with us, did by a set of resolutions in January, in the Year of Our Lord One Thousand Eight Hundred and Forty-Six, dissolve all political connexion with the people of this Republic, returned the power with which it was delegated, and left the people to the government of themselves.

The people of the Republic of Liberia, then, are of right, and in fact, a free, sovereign, and independent State; possessed of all the rights, powers, and functions of government.

In assuming the momentous responsibilities of the position they have taken, the people of this Republic feel justified by the necessities of the case, and with this conviction they throw themselves with confidence upon the candid consideration of the civilized world.

Liberia is not the offspring of grasping ambition, nor the tool of avaricious speculation.

No desire for territorial aggrandizement brought us to these shores; nor do we believe so sordid a motive entered into the high consideration of those who aided us in providing this asylum.

Liberia is an asylum from the most grinding oppression.

In coming to the shores of Africa, we indulged the pleasing hope that we would be permitted to exercise and improve those faculties which impart to man his dignity—to nourish in our hearts the flame of honorable ambition, to cherish and indulge those aspirations, which a beneficent Creator had implanted in every human heart, and to evince to all who despise, ridicule, and oppress our race, that we possess with

them a common nature; are with them susceptible of equal refinement, and capable of equal advancement in all that adorns
and dignifies man.

We were animated with the hope that here we should be at
liberty to train up our children in the way they should go—to
inspire them with the love of an honorable fame, to kindle
within them, the flame of a lofty philanthropy, and to form
strong within them, the principles of humanity, virtue, and religion.

Amongst the strongest motives to leave our native land—to
abandon forever the scenes of our childhood and to sever the
most endeared connexions, was the desire for a retreat where,
free from the agitations of fear and molestation, we could in
composure and security approach in worship, the God of our
fathers.

Thus far our highest hopes have been realized.

Liberia is already the happy home of thousands, who were
once the doomed victims of oppression, and if left unmolested
to go on with her natural and spontaneous growth; if her movements be left free from the paralysing intrigues of jealous, ambitious and unscrupulous avarice, she will throw open wider
and yet a wider door for thousands, who are now looking with
an anxious eye for some land of rest.

Our courts of justice are open equally to the stranger and
the citizen for the redress of grievances, for the remedy of injuries, and for the punishment of crime.

Our numerous and well attended schools attest our efforts, and our desire for the improvement of our children.

Our churches for the worship of our Creator, every where to be seen, bear testimony to our piety, and to our acknowledgment of His Providence.

The native African bowing down with us before the altar of the living God, declares that from us, feeble as we are, the light of Christianity has gone forth, while upon that curse of curses, the slave trade, a deadly blight has fallen as far as our influence extends.

Therefore in the name of humanity, and virtue and religion—in the name of the Great God, our common Creator, and our common Judge, we appeal to the nations of Christendom, and earnestly and respectfully ask of them, that they will regard us with the sympathy and friendly consideration, to which the peculiarities of our condition entitle us, and to extend to us, that comity which marks the friendly intercourse of civilized and independent communities.

Source: The Independent Republic of Liberia; Its Constitution and Declaration of Independence . . . with Other Documents; Issued Chiefly for the Use of the Free People of Color (Philadelphia, 1848), 8–9.

Declaration of Independence of
the Czechoslovak Nation
(October 18, 1918)

At this grave moment, when the Hohenzollerns are offering peace in order to stop the victorious advance of the Allied armies and to prevent the dismemberment of Austria-Hungary and Turkey, and when the Habsburgs are promising the federalization of the Empire and autonomy to the dissatisfied nationalities committed to their rule, we, the Czechoslovak National Council, recognized by the Allied and American Governments as the Provisional Government of the Czechoslovak State and Nation, in complete accord with the declaration of the Czech Deputies made in Prague on January 6, 1918, and realizing that federalization, and still more, autonomy, mean nothing under a Habsburg dynasty, do hereby make and declare this our Declaration of Independence.

We do this because of our belief that no people should be forced to live under a sovereignty they do not recognize, and because of our knowledge and firm conviction that our nation cannot freely develop in a Habsburg mock-federation, which is only a new form of the denationalizing oppression under which we have suffered for the past three hundred years. We consider freedom to be the first pre-requisite for federalization, and believe that the free nations of Central and Eastern Europe may easily federate should they find it necessary.

We make this declaration on the basis of our historic and natural right. We have been an independent state since the seventh century; and, in 1526, as an independent state, consisting of Bohemia, Moravia, and Silesia, we joined with Austria and Hungary in a defensive union against the Turkish danger. We have never voluntarily surrendered our rights as an independent state in this confederation. The Habsburgs broke their compact with our nation by illegally transgressing our rights and violating the Constitution of our state which they had pledged themselves to uphold, and we therefore refuse longer to remain a part of Austria-Hungary in any form.

We claim the right of Bohemia to be re-united with her Slovak brethren of Slovakia, once part of our national state, later torn from our national body, and fifty years ago incorporated into the Hungarian state of the Magyars, who, by their unspeakable violence and ruthless oppression of their subject races have lost all moral and human right to rule anybody but themselves.

The world knows the history of our struggle against the Habsburg oppression, intensified and systematized by the Austro-Hungarian Dualistic Compromise of 1867. This dualism is only a shameless organization of brute force and exploitation of the majority by the minority; it is a political conspiracy of the Germans and Magyars against our own as well as the other Slav and the Latin nations of the Monarchy. The world knows the justice of our claims, which the Habsburgs themselves dared not deny. Francis Joseph, in the most solemn manner repeatedly recognized the sovereign rights of our nation. The Germans and Magyars opposed this recognition, and Austria-Hungary, bowing before the Pan-Germans, became a colony of Germany, and as her vanguard to the east, provoked the last Balkan conflict, as well as the present world-war, which was begun by the Habsburgs alone without the consent of the representatives of the people.

We cannot and will not continue to live under the rule—direct or indirect—of the violators of Belgium, France, and Serbia, the would-be murderers of Russia and Rumania, the murderers of tens of thousands of civilians and soldiers of our blood, and the accomplices in numberless unspeakable crimes committed in this war against humanity by the two degenerate and irresponsible dynasties. We will not remain a part of a State which has no justification for existence, and which, refusing to accept the fundamental principles of modern world-organization, remains only an artificial and immoral political structure, hindering every movement toward democratic and social progress. The Habsburg dynasty, weighed down by a huge inheritance of error and crime, is a perpetual menace to the peace of the world, and we deem it our duty toward humanity and civilization to aid in bringing about its downfall and destruction.

We reject the sacrilegious assertion that the power of the Habsburg and Hohenzollern dynasties is of divine origin; we refuse to recognize the divine right of kings. Our nation elected the Habsburgs to the throne of Bohemia of its own free will and by the same right deposes them. We hereby declare the Habsburg dynasty unworthy of leading our nation, and deny all of their claims to rule in the Czechoslovak Land, which we here and now declare shall henceforth be a free and independent people and nation.

We accept and shall adhere to the ideals of modern democracy, as they have been the ideals of our nation for centuries. We accept the American principles as laid down by President Wilson: the principles of liberated mankind—of the actual equality of nations—and of governments deriving all their just powers from the consent of the governed. We, the nation of Comenius, cannot but accept these principles expressed in the American Declaration of Independence, the principles of Lincoln, and of the Declaration of the Rights of Man and of the Citizen. For these principles our nation shed its blood in the memorable Hussite Wars five hundred years ago, for these same principles, beside her Allies in Russia, Italy, and France, our nation is shedding its blood today.

We shall outline only the main principles of the Constitution of the Czechoslovak Nation; the final decision as to the Constitution itself falls to the legally chosen representatives of the liberated and united people.

The Czechoslovak State shall be a republic. In constant endeavor for progress it will guarantee complete freedom of conscience, religion and science, literature and art, speech, the press and the right of assembly and petition. The Church shall be separated from the state. Our democracy shall rest on universal suffrage; women shall be placed on an equal footing with men, politically, socially, and culturally. The rights of the minority shall be safeguarded by proportional representation; national minorities shall enjoy equal rights. The government shall be parliamentary in form and shall recognize the principles of initiative and referendum. The standing army will be replaced by militia.

The Czechoslovak Nation will carry out far-reaching social and economic reforms; the large estates will be redeemed for home colonization, patents of nobility will be abolished. Our nation will assume its part of the Austro-Hungarian pre-war debt;—the debts for this war we leave to those who incurred them.

In its foreign policy the Czechoslovak Nation will accept its full share of responsibility in the reorganization of Eastern Europe. It accepts fully the democratic and social principle of nationalism and subscribes to the doctrine that all covenants and treaties shall be entered into openly and frankly without secret diplomacy.

Our constitution shall provide an efficient, rational, and just government, which will exclude all special privileges and prohibit class legislation.

Democracy has defeated theocratic autocracy. Militarism is overcome,—democracy is victorious;—on the basis of democracy mankind will be reorganized. The forces of darkness have served the victory of light,—the longed-for age of humanity is dawning.

We believe in democracy,—we believe in liberty,—and liberty evermore.

Given in Paris, on the 18th day of October 1918.

Professor Thomas G. Masaryk

Prime Minister and Minister of Finance

General Dr. Milan R. Stefanik

Minister of National Defense

Dr. Edward Benes

Minister of Foreign

Affairs and of Interior

Source: George J. Kovtun, *The Czechoslovak Declaration of Independence: A History of the Document* (Washington, D.C., 1985), 54–56.

Declaration of Independence of the Democratic Republic of Viet Nam (September 2, 1945)

All men are created equal. They are endowed by their Creator with certain inalienable rights, among these are Life, Liberty and the pursuit of Happiness.

This immortal statement was made in the Declaration of Independence of the United States of America in 1776. In a broader sense, this means: All the peoples on earth are equal from birth, all the peoples have a right to live, to be happy and free.

The Declaration of the French Revolution made in 1791 on the Rights of Man and the Citizen also states: "All men are born free and with equal rights, and must always remain free and have equal rights."

Those are undeniable truths.

Nevertheless, for more than eighty years, the French imperialists, abusing the standard of Liberty, Equality and Fraternity, have violated our Fatherland and oppressed our fellow-citizens. Their have acted contrary to the ideals of humanity and justice.

In the field of politics, they have deprived our people of every democratic liberty.

They have enforced inhuman laws; they have set up three distinct political regimes in the North, the Centre and the South of Viet Nam in order to wreck our national unity and prevent our people from being united.

They have built more prisons than schools. They have mercilessly slain our patriots; they have drowned our uprisings in rivers of blood.

They have fettered public opinion; they have practised obscurantism against our people.

To weaken our race they have forced us to use opium and alcohol.

In the field of economics, they have fleeced us to the backbone, impoverished our people and devastated our land.

They have robbed us of our ricefields, our mines, our forests and our raw materials. They have monopolized the issuing of bank-notes and the export trade.

They have invented numerous unjustifiable taxes and reduced our people, especially our peasantry, to a state of extreme poverty.

They have hampered the prospering of our national bourgeoisie; they have mercilessly exploited our workers.

In the autumn of 1940 when the Japanese fascists violated Indo-China's territory to establish new bases in their fight against the Allies, the French imperialists went down on their bended knees and handed over our country to them.

Thus, from that date, our people were subjected to the double yoke of the French and the Japanese. Their sufferings and miseries increased. The result was that from the end of last year to the beginning of this year, from Quang Tri province to the North of Viet Nam, more than two millions of our fellow-citizens died from starvation. On the 9th of March, the French troops were disarmed by the Japanese. The French colonialists either fled or surrendered, showing that not only were they incapable of "protecting" us, but that, in the span of five years, they had twice sold our country to the Japanese.

On several occasions before the 9th of March, the Viet Minh League urged the French to ally themselves with it against the Japanese. Instead of agreeing to this proposal, the French colonialists so intensified their terrorist activities against the Viet Minh members that before fleeing they massacred a great number of our political prisoners at Yen Bay and Cao Bang.

Notwithstanding all this, our fellow-citizens have always manifested towards the French a tolerant and humane attitude. Even after the Japanese putsch of March 1945, the Viet Minh League helped many Frenchmen to cross the frontier, rescued some of them from Japanese jails and protected French lives and property.

From the autumn of 1940, our country had in fact ceased to be a French colony and had become a Japanese possession.

After the Japanese had surrendered to the Allies, our whole

people rose to regain our national sovereignty and to found the Democratic Republic of Viet Nam.

The truth is that we have wrested our independence from the Japanese and not from the French.

The French have fled, the Japanese have capitulated, Emperor Bao Dai has abdicated. Our people have broken the chains which for nearly a century have fettered them and have won independence for the Fatherland. Our people at the same time have overthrown the monarchic regime that has reigned supreme for dozens of centuries. In its place has been established the present Democratic Republic.

For these reasons we, members of the Provisional Government, representing the whole Vietnamese people, declare that from now on we break off all relations of a colonial character with France; we repeal all the international obligation that France has so far subscribed to on behalf of Viet Nam and we abolish all the special rights the French have unlawfully acquired in our Fatherland.

The whole Vietnamese people, animated by a common purpose, are determined to fight to the bitter end against any attempt by the French colonialists to reconquer their country.

We are convinced that the Allied nations which at Teheran and San Francisco have acknowledged the principles of self-determination and equality of nations, will not refuse to acknowledge the independence of Viet Nam.

A people who have courageously opposed French domination for more than eighty years, a people who have fought side by side with the Allies against the fascists during these last years, such a people must be free and independent.

For these reasons, we, members of the Provisional Government of the Democratic Republic of Viet Nam, solemnly declare to the world that Viet Nam has the right to be a free and independent country—and in fact it is so already. The entire Vietnamese people are determined to mobilize all their physical and mental strength, to sacrifice their lives and property in order to safeguard their independence and liberty.

_____

Source: Ho Chi Minh, *Selected Works,* 4 vols. (Hanoi, 1960–1962), III, 17–21.

Declaration of the Establishment of the State of Israel (May 14, 1948)

ERETZ ISRAEL* was the birthplace of the Jewish people. Here their spiritual, religious and political identity was shaped. Here they first attained to statehood, created cultural values of national and universal significance and gave to the world the eternal Book of Books.

After being forcibly exiled from their land, the people kept faith with it throughout their Dispersion and never ceased to pray and hope for their return to it and for the restoration in it of their political freedom.

Impelled by this historic and traditional attachment, Jews strove in every successive generation to re-establish themselves in their ancient homeland. In recent decades they returned in their masses. Pioneers, *ma'pilim*† and defenders, they made deserts bloom, revived the Hebrew language, built villages and towns, and created a thriving community controlling its own economy and culture, loving peace but knowing how to defend itself, bringing the blessings of progress to all the country's inhabitants, and aspiring towards independent nationhood.

---

* The Land of Israel.

† Immigrants coming to Eretz-Israel in defiance of restrictive legislation.

In the year 5657 (1897), at the summons of the spiritual father of the Jewish State, Theodore Herzl, the First Zionist Congress convened and proclaimed the right of the Jewish people to national rebirth in its own country.

This right was recognized in the Balfour Declaration of the 2nd November, 1917, and re-affirmed in the Mandate of the League of Nations which, in particular, gave international sanction to the historic connection between the Jewish people and Eretz-Israel and to the right of the Jewish people to rebuild its National Home.

The catastrophe which recently befell the Jewish people—the massacre of millions of Jews in Europe—was another clear demonstration of the urgency of solving the problem of its homelessness by re-establishing in Eretz-Israel the Jewish State, which would open the gates of the homeland wide to every Jew and confer upon the Jewish people the status of a fully-privileged member of the comity of nations.

Survivors of the Nazi holocaust in Europe, as well as Jews from other parts of the world, continued to migrate to Eretz-Israel, undaunted by difficulties, restrictions and dangers, and never ceased to assert their right to a life of dignity, freedom and honest toil in their national homeland.

In the Second World War, the Jewish community of this country contributed its full share to the struggle of the freedom- and peace-loving nations against the forces of Nazi wickedness and, by the blood of its soldiers and its war effort, gained the right to be reckoned among the peoples who founded the United Nations.

On the 29th November, 1947, the United Nations General Assembly passed a resolution calling for the establishment of a Jewish State in Eretz-Israel; the General Assembly required the inhabitants of Eretz-Israel to take such steps as were necessary on their part for the implementation of that resolution. This recognition by the United Nations of the right of the Jewish people to establish their State is irrevocable.

This right is the natural right of the Jewish people to be masters of their own fate, like all other nations, in their own sovereign State.

Accordingly we, members of the People's Council, representatives of the Jewish community of Eretz-Israel and of the Zionist movement, are here assembled on the day of the termination of the British Mandate over Eretz-Israel and, by virtue of our natural and historic right and on the strength of the resolution of the United Nations General Assembly, hereby declare the establishment of a Jewish state in Eretz-Israel, to be known as the State of Israel.

WE DECLARE that, with effect from the moment of the termination of the Mandate, being tonight, the eve of Sabbath, the 6th Iyar, 5708 (15th May, 1948), until the establishment of the elected, regular authorities of the State in accordance with the Constitution which shall be adopted by the Elected Constituent Assembly not later than the 1st October 1948, the People's Council shall act as a Provisional Council of State, and its executive organ, the People's Administration, shall be the Provisional Government of the Jewish State, to be called "Israel".

The State of Israel will be open for Jewish immigration and for the Ingathering of the Exiles; it will foster the development of the country for the benefit of all inhabitants; it will be based on freedom, justice and peace as envisaged by the prophets of Israel; it will ensure complete equality of social and political rights to all its inhabitants irrespective of religion, race or sex; it will guarantee freedom of religion, conscience, language, education and culture; it will safeguard the Holy Places of all religions; and it will be faithful to the principles of the Charter of the United Nations.

The State of Israel is prepared to cooperate with the agencies and representatives of the United Nations in implementing the resolution of the General Assembly of the 29th November, 1947, and will take steps to bring about the economic union of the whole of Eretz-Israel.

We appeal to the United Nations to assist the Jewish people in the building-up of its State and to receive the State of Israel into the comity of nations.

We appeal—in the very midst of the onslaught launched against us now for months—to the Arab inhabitants of the State of Israel to preserve peace and participate in the upbuilding of the State on the basis of full and equal citizenship and due representation in all its provisional and permanent institutions.

We extend our hand to all neighbouring states and their peoples in an offer of peace and good neighbourliness, and appeal to them to establish bonds of cooperation and mutual help with the sovereign Jewish people settled in its own land. The State of Israel is prepared to do its share in a common effort for the advancement of the entire Middle East.

We appeal to the Jewish people throughout the Diaspora to rally round the Jews of Eretz-Israel in the tasks of immigration and upbuilding and to stand by them in the great struggle for the realization of the age-old dream—the redemption of Israel.

Placing our trust in the Almighty, we affix our signatures to this proclamation at this session of the Provisional Council of State, on the soil of the homeland, in the city of Tel-Aviv, on this Sabbath eve, the 5th day of Iyar, 5708 (14th May, 1948).

Source: Independence Documents of the World, ed. Albert P. Blaustein, Jay Sigler, and Benjamin R. Beede, 2 vols. (New York, 1977), I, 371.

The Unilateral Declaration of Independence (Southern Rhodesia) (November 11, 1965)

Whereas in the course of human affairs history has shown that it may become necessary for a people to resolve the political affiliations which have connected them with another people and to assume amongst other nations the separate and equal status to which they are entitled:

And whereas in such event a respect for the opinions of mankind requires them to declare to other nations the causes which impel them to assume full responsibility for their own affairs:

Now therefore, we, the Government of Rhodesia, do hereby declare:

That it is an indisputable and accepted historic fact that since 1923 the Government of Rhodesia have exercised the powers of self-government and have been responsible for the progress, development and welfare of their people;

That the people of Rhodesia having demonstrated their loyalty to the Crown and to their kith and kin in the United Kingdom and elsewhere through two world wars, and having prepared to shed their blood and give of what their substance in they believed to be the mutual interests of freedom-loving people, now see all that they have cherished, about to be shattered on the rocks of expediency;

That the people of Rhodesia have witnessed a process which is destructive of those very precepts upon which civilization in a primitive country has been built; they have seen the principles of Western democracy, responsible government and moral standards crumble elsewhere; nevertheless they have remained steadfast;

That the people of Rhodesia fully support the requests of their Government for sovereign independence but have witnessed the consistent refusal of the Government of the United Kingdom to accede to their entreaties;

That the Government of the United Kingdom have thus demonstrated that they are not prepared to grant sovereign independence to Rhodesia on terms acceptable to the people of Rhodesia, thereby persisting in maintaining an unwarrantable jurisdiction over Rhodesia, obstructing laws and treaties with other states and the conduct of affairs with other nations and refusing assent to laws necessary for the public good; all this to the detriment of the future peace, prosperity and good government of Rhodesia;

That the Government of Rhodesia have for a long period patiently and in good faith negotiated with the Government of the United Kingdom for the removal of the remaining limitations placed upon them and for the grant of sovereign independence;

That in the belief that procrastination and delay strike at and injure the very life of the nation, the Government of Rhodesia consider it essential that Rhodesia should attain, without delay, sovereign independence, the justice of which is beyond question;

Now therefore, we, the Government of Rhodesia, in humble submission to Almighty God who controls the destinies of nations, conscious that the people of Rhodesia have always shown unswerving loyalty and devotion to Her Majesty the Queen and earnestly praying that we and the people of Rhodesia will not be hindered in our determination to continue exercising our undoubted right to demonstrate the same loyalty and devotion, and seeking to promote the common good so that the dignity and freedom of all men may be assured, do, by this Proclamation, adopt, enact and give to the people of Rhodesia the Constitution annexed hereto.

God save the Queen.

Given under Our Hand at Salisbury, this eleventh day of November in The Year of Our Lord one thousand nine hundred and sixty-five.

Source: Independence Documents of the World, ed. Albert P. Blaustein, Jay Sigler, and Benjamin R. Beede, 2 vols. (New York, 1977), II, 587.

Notes

Acknowledgments

Index

Notes

Introduction

1. Jefferson to Roger C. Weightman, June 24, 1826, in *The Writings of Thomas Jefferson,* ed. Andrew A. Lipscomb and Albert Ellery Bergh, 20 vols. (Washington, D.C., 1903–1904), XVI, 181–182.

2. J. Jefferson Looney, "Thomas Jefferson's Last Letter," *Virginia Magazine of History and Biography,* 112 (2004), 178–184. On Jefferson's interest in wine see especially James M. Gabler, *Passions: The Wines and Travels of Thomas Jefferson* (Baltimore, 1995).

3. Pauline Maier, *American Scripture: Making the Declaration of Independence* (New York, 1997), 154–208.

4. For comparable treatments of other works see Isabel Hofmeyr, *The Portable Bunyan: A Transnational History of "The Pilgrim's Progress"* (Princeton, 2004); Esteban Buch, *Beethoven's Ninth: A Political History* (Chicago, 2003). See also Franco Moretti, *Atlas of the European Novel, 1800–1900* (London, 1998).

5. *Las Actas de Independencia de América,* ed. Javier Malagón (Washington, D.C., 1955).

6. *Independence Documents of the World,* ed. Albert P. Blaustein, Jay Sigler, and Benjamin R. Beede, 2 vols. (New York, 1977).

7. See, though, the brief but insightful essay by Charles C. Griffin, "América y sus Actas de Independencia," in *Las Actas de Independencia de América,* ed. Malagón, xvii–xx.

8. Most notably Herbert Friedenwald, *The Declaration of Independence, An Interpretation and an Analysis* (New York, 1904); John Hazelton, *The Declaration of Independence: Its History* (New York, 1906); Carl L. Becker, *The Declaration of Independence: A Study in the History of Political Ideas,* rev. ed. (New York, 1942); Julian P. Boyd, *The Declaration of*

Independence: The Evolution of the Text, ed. Gerard W. Gawalt (Washington, D.C., 1999); Morton White, *The Philosophy of the American Revolution* (New York, 1978); Garry Wills, *Inventing America: Jefferson's Declaration of Independence* (New York, 1978); Jay Fliegelman, *Declaring Independence: Jefferson, Natural Language, and the Culture of Performance* (Stanford, 1993); Maier, *American Scripture;* Allen Jayne, *Jefferson's Declaration of Independence: Origins, Philosophy and Theology* (Lexington, KY, 1998).

9. See, for example, Charles D. Desbler, "How The Declaration Was Received in the Old Thirteen," *Harper's New Monthly Magazine,* 85 (July 1892), 165–187; Philip F. Detweiler, "The Changing Reputation of the Declaration of Independence: The First Fifty Years," *William and Mary Quarterly,* 3rd ser., 19 (1962), 557–574; *We, the Other People: Alternative Declarations of Independence by Labor Groups, Farmers, Woman's Rights Advocates, Socialists, and Blacks, 1829–1975,* ed. Philip S. Foner (Urbana, 1976); Merrill D. Peterson, *"This Grand Pertinacity": Abraham Lincoln and the Declaration of Independence* (Fort Wayne, 1991); Maier, *American Scripture,* 170–215; and many of the essays in Scott Douglas Gerber, ed., *The Declaration of Independence: Origins and Impact* (Washington, D.C., 2002).

10. Though there is much useful material toward such an enterprise in Richard B. Morris, *The Emerging Nations and the American Revolution* (New York, 1970), and in "Interpreting the Declaration of Independence by Translation: A Round Table," *Journal of American History,* 85 (1999), 1280–1460. For summaries of their findings see Morris, "The Declaration was Proclaimed but Few in Europe Listened at First," *Smithsonian,* 6, 4 (July 1975), 30–36; David Thelen, "Reception of the Declaration of Independence," in Gerber, ed., *The Declaration of Independence: Origins and Impact,* 191–212.

11. The burgeoning field of Atlantic history traces these interactions, mostly in the period c. 1492–1825: Bernard Bailyn, *Atlantic History: Concept and Contours* (Cambridge, MA, 2005).

12. Eric Foner, "American Freedom in a Global Age," *American Historical Review,* 106 (2001), 1–16; Thomas Bender, ed., *Rethinking American*

History in a Global Age (Berkeley, 2002); Bender, *A Nation among Nations: America's Place in World History* (New York, 2006).

13. C. A. Bayly, *The Birth of the Modern World, 1780–1914* (Oxford, 2004), 1.

14. A. G. Hopkins, ed., *Globalization in World History* (London, 2002); David Armitage, "Is There a Pre-History of Globalization?" in Deborah Cohen and Maura O'Connor, eds., *Comparison and History: Europe in Cross-National Perspective* (London, 2004), 165–176; Sugata Bose, *A Hundred Horizons: The Indian Ocean in an Age of Global Empire* (Cambridge, MA, 2006).

15. H. V. Bowen, "British Conceptions of Global Empire, 1756–83," *Journal of Imperial and Commonwealth History*, 26 (1998), 1–27.

16. Burke to William Robertson, June 9, 1777, in *The Correspondence of Edmund Burke*, 10 vols., ed. T. W. Copeland et al. (Cambridge, 1958–1978), III, 350–351.

17. Adam Smith, *An Inquiry into the Nature and Causes of the Wealth of Nations* (1776), ed. R. H. Campbell and A. S. Skinner, 2 vols. (Oxford, 1976), II, 947.

18. Robertson to [Sir Robert Murray Keith?], March 8, 1784, British Library Add. MS 35350, fol. 70v.

19. Richard B. Sheridan, "The British Credit Crisis of 1772 and the American Colonies," *Journal of Economic History*, 20 (1960), 161–186; Emma Rothschild, "Globalization and the Return of History," *Foreign Policy*, 115 (Summer 1999), 106–116; Rothschild, "The Last Empire: Security and Globalization in Historical Perspective," *Jerome E. Levy Occasional Paper*, 5 (Annapolis, 2002); Marc Aronson, *The Real Revolution: The Global Story of American Independence* (New York, 2005); Bender, *A Nation among Nations*, 77–78.

20. Jeremy Bentham, *An Introduction to the Principles of Morals and Legislation* (1780/89), ed. J. H. Burns and H. L. A. Hart, Intro. F. Rosen (Oxford, 1996), 6, 296; Hidemi Suganami, "A Note on the Origin of the Word 'International,'" *British Journal of International Studies*, 4 (1978), 226–232.

21. "Dunlap, John (1747–1812)," in John A. Garraty and Mark C.

Carnes, gen. eds., *American National Biography,* 24 vols. (New York, 1999), VII, 87–89.

22. Frederick R. Goff, *The John Dunlap Broadside: The First Printing of the Declaration of Independence* (Washington, D.C., 1976), 9–10 (noting that twelve out of seventeen copies examined were printed on Dutch paper), 11, 14; John Bidwell, "Printers' Supplies and Capitalization," in Hugh Amory and David D. Hall, eds., *A History of the Book in America,* I: *The Colonial Book in the Atlantic World* (Cambridge, 2000), 168–171.

23. "Syng, Philip, Jr. (1703–1789)," in Garraty and Carnes, eds., *American National Biography,* XXI, 232–233; Richard Lyman Bushman, "The Complexity of Silver," in Jeannine Falino and Gerald W. R. Ward, eds., *New England Silver and Silversmithing, 1620–1815, Publications of the Colonial Society of Massachusetts,* 70 (Boston, 2001), 11–13; biographical information on the signers from *Dictionary of American Biography,* 22 vols. (New York, 1928–1958), and Garraty and Carnes, eds., *American National Biography.*

24. Becker, *The Declaration of Independence,* viii.

25. See generally Mikhail Bakhtin, "The Problem of Speech Genres" (1952–1953), in Bakhtin, *Speech Genres and Other Late Essays,* trans. Vern W. McGee, ed. Caryl Emerson and Michael Holquist (Austin, TX, 1986), 60–102, and Alastair Fowler, *Forms of Literature: An Introduction to the Theory of Genres and Modes* (Cambridge, MA, 1982).

26. Keith Michael Baker, "The Idea of a Declaration of Rights," in Dale Van Kley, ed., *The French Idea of Freedom: The Old Regime and the Declaration of Rights of 1789* (Stanford, 1994), 154–196; Christine Fauré, *Ce que déclarer des droits veut dire: histoires* (Paris, 1997).

27. See Janet Lyon, *Manifestoes: Provocations of the Modern* (Ithaca, 1999); Jeffrey M. Encke, "Manifestos: A Social History of Proclamation" (Ph.D. thesis, Columbia University, 2002), though neither deals with diplomatic manifestos, arguably the most widespread form of the genre in the period before the *Communist Manifesto* of 1848.

28. "L'indépendance des Anglo-Américains est l'événement le plus

propre à accélérer la révolution qui doit ramener le bonheur sur la terre. C'est au sein de cette République naissante que sont déposés les vrais trésors qui enrichiront le monde": Abbé Genty, quoted in Daniel Mornet, *Les origines intellectuelles de la Révolution Française (1715–1787),* 2nd ed. (Paris, 1934), 396–397.

29. Charles Warren, "Fourth of July Myths," *William and Mary Quarterly,* 3rd ser., 3 (1945), 247–248; Jack N. Rakove, "The Decision for American Independence: A Reconstruction," *Perspectives in American History,* 10 (1976), 250–253, 265; Jefferson to Richard Henry Lee, July 8, 1776, in *The Papers of Thomas Jefferson,* gen. ed. Julian P. Boyd, 31 vols. to date (Princeton, 1950–), I, 455.

30. *Pennsylvania Evening Post,* August 15, 1776, quoted in Stephen E. Lucas, "Justifying America: The Declaration of Independence as a Rhetorical Document," in Thomas W. Benson, ed., *American Rhetoric: Context and Criticism* (Carbondale, 1989), 119; *I [blank] do acknowledge the UNITED STATES of AMERICA to be Free, Independent and Sovereign States . . .* (n.p., n.d [Philadelphia, 1776]).

31. Colin Warbrick, "States and Recognition in International Law," in Malcolm D. Evans, ed., *International Law* (Oxford, 2003), 220–221.

32. Charles S. Maier, *Among Empires: American Ascendancy and Its Predecessors* (Cambridge, MA, 2006), brilliantly captures the ambivalences of the relationship between states and empires as overlapping forms of polity, social structure, and economic organization.

33. Akira Iriye, *Global Community: The Role of International Organizations in the Making of the Modern World* (Berkeley, 2002); Alfred D. Chandler, Jr., and Bruce Mazlish, eds., *Leviathans: Multinational Corporations and the New Global History* (Cambridge, 2005).

34. Ernest Gellner, *Nations and Nationalism* (London, 1983), 6–7.

35. For important pointers see Charles Tilly, ed., *The Formation of National States in Western Europe* (Princeton, 1975); Hedley Bull and Adam Watson, eds., *The Expansion of International Society* (Oxford, 1984); Frederick Cooper, "States, Empires, and Political Imagination," in Cooper, *Colonialism in Question: Theory, Knowledge, History* (Berkeley, 2005), 153–203.

36. Jefferson to Henry Lee, May 8, 1825, in *The Writings of Thomas Jefferson,* eds. Lipscomb and Bergh, XVI, 118.

37. Edmund C. Burnett, "The Name 'United States of America,'" *American Historical Review,* 31 (1925), 79–81. For a slightly earlier, informal usage of the term see Republicus, "To the People of Pennsylvania" (June 29, 1776), in *American Archives: Fourth Series . . . From the King's Message to Parliament, of March 7, 1774, to the Declaration of Independence by the United States,* ed. Peter Force, 6 vols. (Washington, D.C., 1833–1846), VI, 1131.

1. *The World in the Declaration of Independence*

1. Abraham Lincoln, "Speech at Springfield, Illinois" (June 26, 1857), in *The Collected Works of Abraham Lincoln,* ed. Roy P. Basler, 9 vols. (New Brunswick, NJ, 1953–1955), II, 406.

2. Wilbur Samuel Howell, "The Declaration of Independence and Eighteenth-Century Logic," *William and Mary Quarterly,* 3rd ser., 18 (1961), 463–484.

3. On these prevailing assumptions as they were deployed by Americans see Peter Onuf and Nicholas Onuf, *Federal Union, Modern World: The Law of Nations in an Age of Revolutions, 1776–1814* (Madison, 1993); David C. Hendrickson, *Peace Pact: The Lost World of the American Founding* (Lawrence, KS, 2003), chaps. 7–16.

4. Pauline Maier, *American Scripture: Making the Declaration of Independence* (New York, 1997), 51–57.

5. William Blackstone, *Commentaries on the Laws of England,* 4 vols. (London, 1765–1769), III, 293.

6. [Robert Plumer Ward,] *An Enquiry into the Manner in which the Different Wars in Europe Have Commenced, During the Last Two Centuries: To which Are Added the Authorities upon the Nature of a Modern Declaration* (London, 1805), 3.

7. Carl-August Fleischhauer, "Declaration," in *Encyclopedia of Public International Law,* gen. ed. Rudolf Bernhardt, 12 vols. to date (Amsterdam, 1982–), VII, 67.

8. "A Declaration by the Representatives of the United Colonies . . . Seting Forth the Causes and Necessity of Their Taking up Arms" (July 6, 1775), in *A Decent Respect to the Opinions of Mankind: Congressional State Papers, 1774–1776,* ed. James H. Hutson (Washington, D.C., 1976), 91–97. For a more extensive treatment of the texts of this declaration see *The Papers of Thomas Jefferson,* gen. ed. Julian P. Boyd, 31 vols. to date (Princeton, 1950–), I, 187–219.

9. "A Declaration by the Representatives of the United Colonies . . . Seting Forth the Causes and Necessity of Their Taking up Arms" (July 6, 1775); "To the Inhabitants of the Colonies . . ." (October 27, 1774), in *A Decent Respect to the Opinions of Mankind,* ed. Hutson, 35.

10. Jerrilyn Greene Marston, *King and Congress: The Transfer of Political Legitimacy, 1774–1776* (Princeton, 1987), 206–223.

11. Thomas Jefferson, "Notes of Proceedings in the Continental Congress" (June 7–August 1, 1776), in *The Papers of Thomas Jefferson,* ed. Boyd, I, 311.

12. John Adams to Horatio Gates, March 23, 1776, in *Letters of Delegates to Congress, 1774–1789,* gen. ed. Paul H. Smith, 26 vols. to date (Washington, D.C., 1976–), III, 431, referring to the Prohibitory Act (16 Geo. III, c. 5).

13. Richard Henry Lee, "Resolution of Independence" (June 7, 1776), in *Journals of the Continental Congress, 1774–1789,* ed. Worthington C. Ford, 5 vols. (Washington, D.C., 1904–1906), V, 425–426.

14. Felix Gilbert, *To the Farewell Address: Ideas of Early American Foreign Policy* (Princeton, 1961), 44–54. The treaty was modeled in part on examples found in the copy of *A Compleat Collection of All the Articles and Clauses which Relate to the Marine, in the Several Treaties Now Subsisting Between Great Britain and Other Kingdoms and States,* ed. Henry Edmunds and William Harris (London, 1760), now in the Houghton Library, Harvard University (call number *EC7 Ed596 741 ed).

15. Merrill Jensen, *The Articles of Confederation: An Interpretation of the Social-Constitutional History of the American Revolution, 1774–1781,* new ed. (Madison, 1970), 175–176, 263, 264–265, 266.

16. John Adams to James Warren, October 7, 1775, in *The Warren-Adams Letters: Being Chiefly a Correspondence among John Adams, Samuel Adams, and James Warren,* ed. Worthington C. Ford, 2 vols. (Boston, 1917–1925), I, 127–128.

17. Richard Henry Lee to Patrick Henry, April 20, 1776, in *The Letters of Richard Henry Lee,* ed. James Curtis Ballagh, 2 vols. (New York, 1911–1914), I, 178.

18. Thomas Paine, *Common Sense* (Philadelphia, 1776), 77–78.

19. North Carolina Instructions (April 12, 1776); Instructions for the Delegates of Charlotte County, Virginia (April 23, 1776); Virginia Instructions (May 15, 1776); "Meeting of the Inhabitants of the Town of Malden" (May 27, 1776); Connecticut Instructions (June 14, 1776), in *American Archives: Fourth Series . . . From the King's Message to Parliament, of March 7, 1774, to the Declaration of Independence by the United States,* ed. Peter Force, 6 vols. (Washington, D.C., 1833–1846), V, 1322, 1035; VI, 461, 602, 868.

20. Quentin Skinner, "From the State of Princes to the Person of the State," in Skinner, *Visions of Politics,* II: *Renaissance Virtues* (Cambridge, 2002), 368–413; Skinner, *Liberty before Liberalism* (Cambridge, 1998); J. R. Pole, "The Politics of the Word 'State' and Its Relation to American Sovereignty," *Parliaments, Estates and Representation,* 8 (1998), 1–10.

21. David Ramsay, *An Oration on the Advantages of American Independence* (Charleston, SC, 1778), 12.

22. Frederick G. Whelan, "Vattel's Doctrine of the State," *History of Political Thought,* 9 (1988), 59–90.

23. Emer de Vattel, *Le Droit des gens, ou principes de la loi naturelle* (Neuchâtel, 1758); Charles G. Fenwick, "The Authority of Vattel," *American Political Science Review,* 7 (1913), 370–424; ibid., 8 (1914), 375–392; F. S. Ruddy, *International Law in the Enlightenment: The Background of Emmerich de Vattel's Le Droit des Gens* (Dobbs Ferry, 1975); Emmanuelle Jouannet, *Emer de Vattel et l'émergence doctrinale du droit international classique* (Paris, 1998).

24. Emer de Vattel, *Le Droit des gens, ou principes de la loi naturelle,* ed. C. G. F. Dumas, 2 vols. (Amsterdam, 1775), I, 12, 2, 6, 7, 8 (my translations). Vattel does not distinguish conceptually or formally between "les Nations, ou les Etats souverains": *Le Droit des gens,* I, 2.

25. Emer de Vattel, *The Law of Nations, or, Principles of the Law of Nature, Applied to the Conduct and Affairs of Nations and Sovereigns* (London, 1760), xi.

26. Ian Brownlie, *Principles of Public International Law,* 4th ed. (Oxford, 1990), 73–74.

27. William Bradford to James Madison, October 17, 1774, in *The Papers of James Madison,* gen. eds. William T. Hutchinson and William M. E. Rachal, 17 vols. (Chicago, 1962–1991), I, 126. "Barlemaqui" was the Swiss theorist of natural law Jean Jacques Burlamaqui, on whom see especially Morton White, *The Philosophy of the American Revolution* (New York, 1978).

28. Franklin to Dumas, December 9, 1775, in *The Papers of Benjamin Franklin,* gen. eds. Leonard W. Labaree et al., 37 vols. to date (New Haven, 1959–), XXII, 287. Library Company of Philadelphia, call number Rare E Vatt 303. Q; Houghton Library, Harvard University, call number *AC7 F8545 Zz775v.

29. A. A. M. Duncan, *The Nation of Scots and the Declaration of Arbroath (1320)* (London, 1970), 34–37; J. R. Philip, "Sallust and the Declaration of Arbroath," *Scottish Historical Review,* 26 (1947), 75–78.

30. [Burns Federation,] *Declaration of Independence 1320* (n.p., n.d.); [Scots Secretariat,] *Scotland's Scrap of Paper: Full Text of Treaty of Union of 1707, with Notes, Declaration of Independence, Radical Rising 1820, Policy of Scottish Nationalism* (Penicuik, 1975); Edward J. Cowan, *"For Freedom Alone": The Declaration of Arbroath, 1320* (East Linton, 2003), 5, 114; United States, 105th Congress, 2nd Session, Senate Resolution 155 (March 19, 1998).

31. "Edict of the States General of the United Netherlands by which they Declare that the King of Spain has Forfeited the Sovereignty and Government of the Afore-said Netherlands" (July 26, 1581), in *Texts con-*

cerning the Revolt of the Netherlands, ed. E. H. Kossmann and A. F. Mellink (Cambridge, 1974), 224.

32. "Het is de parodie van het stuk, dat onze voorzaeten deeden uitgeeven tegens koning Philips de tweede": William V, prince of Orange, to Hendrik Fagel, August 20, 1776, in *Archives ou correspondance inédite de la maison d'Orange-Nassau,* ed. F. J. L. Krämer, 5th ser., 3 vols. (Leiden, 1910–1915), I, 449, quoted in J. M. Schulte Nordholt, *The Dutch Republic and American Independence,* trans. Herbert H. Rowen (Chapel Hill, 1982), 221.

33. J. P. A. Coopmans, "Het Plakkaat van Verlatinge (1581) en de Declaration of Independence (1776)," *Bijdragen en Mededelingen betreffende de Geschiedenis der Nederlanden,* 98 (1983), 540–567; Stephen E. Lucas, "The 'Plakkaat van Verlatinge': A Neglected Model for the American Declaration of Independence," in Rosemarijn Hoefte, Johanna C. Kardux, and Hans Bak, eds., *Connecting Cultures: The Netherlands in Five Centuries of Transatlantic Exchange* (Amsterdam, 1994), 187–207.

34. William E. Griffis, *The Influence of the Netherlands in the Making of the English Commonwealth and the American Republic* (Boston, 1891), 17, 30, 33; "The Dutch Declaration of Independence," *Old South Leaflets,* 72 (Boston, 1896); Wijnand W. Mijnhardt, "The Declaration of Independence and the Dutch Legacy" (paper presented at the Eleventh Conference of the International Society for Eighteenth-Century Studies, University of California Los Angeles, August 2003).

35. See generally Jack N. Rakove, "The Decision for Independence: A Reconstruction," *Perspectives in American History,* 10 (1976), 217–275.

36. Jefferson, "Notes of Proceedings in the Continental Congress," in *The Papers of Thomas Jefferson,* ed. Boyd, I, 310; James H. Hutson, "The Partition Treaty and the Declaration of American Independence," *Journal of American History,* 58 (1971–1972), 875–896.

37. John Dickinson, "Notes for a Speech in Congress" (July 1, 1776), in *Letters of Delegates to Congress, 1774–1789,* ed. Smith, IV, 355.

38. Benjamin Rush to Charles Lee, July 23, 1776, in *Letters of Delegates to Congress, 1774–1789,* ed. Smith, IV, 528.

39. Thadd E. Hall, *France and the Eighteenth-Century Corsican Question* (New York, 1971); George P. Anderson, "Pascal Paoli, An Inspiration to the Sons of Liberty," *Publications of the Colonial Society of Massachusetts*, 26 (1924–1926), 180–210.

40. Piotr S. Wandycz, "The American Revolution and the Partitions of Poland," in Jaroslaw Pelenski, ed., *The American and European Revolutions, 1776–1848: Sociopolitical and Ideological Aspects* (Iowa City, 1980), 95–110.

41. [Daniel Leonard,] *Massachusettensis* (n.p., n.d. [Boston, 1775]), 63; Richard Henry Lee to Patrick Henry, April 20, 1776, in *Letters of Richard Henry Lee*, ed. Ballagh, I, 176.

42. Thomas Paine, *The American Crisis*, III (April 19, 1777), in Paine, *Collected Writings*, ed. Eric Foner (New York, 1995), 123–124.

43. Jefferson, "Notes of Proceedings in the Continental Congress," in *The Papers of Thomas Jefferson*, ed. Boyd, I, 312.

44. G. C. Gibbs, "The Dutch Revolt and the American Revolution," in Robert Oresko, G. C. Gibbs, and H. M. Scott, eds., *Royal and Republican Sovereignty in Early Modern Europe: Essays in Honour of Ragnhild Hatton* (Cambridge, 1997), 609–637. For a contemporary parallel see the fictional dialogue *Entretiens de Guillaume de Nassau, Prince d'Orange, et du général Montgommery sur la révolution ancienne des Pays-Bas, & les affaires actuelles d'Amérique* (London, 1776).

45. Abigail Adams to John Adams, April 23, 1781, in *Adams Family Correspondence*, ed. L. H. Butterfield et al., 4 vols. (Cambridge, MA, 1963–1973), IV, 104.

46. [John Adams,] *A Collection of State-Papers, Relative to the Acknowledgement of the Sovereignity [sic] of the United States of America* (The Hague, 1782), 8.

47. Anglo-Spanish Treaty of 1667, in *A Compleat Collection of All the Articles and Clauses which Relate to the Marine*, ed. Edmunds and Harris, 52.

48. Jefferson, "Notes of Proceedings in the Continental Congress," in *The Papers of Thomas Jefferson*, ed. Boyd, I, 312–313.

49. Dickinson, "Notes for a Speech in Congress," in *Letters of Delegates to*

Congress, 1774–1789, ed. Smith, IV, 353, 354; Milton E. Flower, *John Dickinson, Conservative Revolutionary* (Charlottesville, 1983), 161–166.

50. Maier, *American Scripture,* 45.

51. Adams to Abigail Adams, July 3, 1776, in *Adams Family Correspondence,* ed. Butterfield, II, 29–33.

52. The best account of the drafting and editing is now Maier, *American Scripture,* 97–153; see also *The Papers of Thomas Jefferson,* ed. Boyd, I, 413–433; Boyd, *The Declaration of Independence.*

53. Jefferson, First and Third Drafts of the Virginia Constitution (before June 13, 1776), Virginia Constitution (June 19, 1776), in *The Papers of Thomas Jefferson,* ed. Boyd, I, 337–340, 356–357, 377–379.

54. "To the Inhabitants of the Colonies" (October 21, 1774), in *A Decent Respect to the Opinions of Mankind,* ed. Hutson, 35–46.

55. "A Letter to the Inhabitants of Quebec" (October 26, 1774), "Address to the Assembly of Jamaica" (July 25, 1775), "Address to the People of Ireland" (July 28, 1775), in *A Decent Respect to the Opinions of Mankind,* ed. Hutson, 66, 135, 111.

56. Bernard Bailyn, *The Ideological Origins of the American Revolution,* rev. ed. (Cambridge, MA, 1992), 144–159; Ira D. Gruber, "The American Revolution as a Conspiracy: The British View," *William and Mary Quarterly,* 3rd ser., 26 (1969), 360–372.

57. Arthur Young, *Political Essays Concerning the Present State of the British Empire* (London, 1772), 19–20.

58. Paine, *Common Sense,* 57, 60.

59. For discussion of the various charges see Sydney George Fisher, "The Twenty-Eight Charges Against the King in the Declaration of Independence," *Pennsylvania Magazine of History and Biography,* 31 (1907), 257–303; Garry Wills, *Inventing America: Jefferson's Declaration of Independence* (New York, 1978), 65–75; Stephen E. Lucas, "Justifying America: The Declaration of Independence as a Rhetorical Document," in Thomas W. Benson, ed., *American Rhetoric: Context and Criticism* (Carbondale, 1989), 96–110; Maier, *American Scripture,* 105–123.

60. "To the Inhabitants of the Colonies" (October 21, 1774), in *A Decent Respect to the Opinions of Mankind,* ed. Hutson, 35–46.

61. [Thomas Jefferson,] *A Summary View of the Rights of British America* (Williamsburg, Va., 1774), 5, 8, 11; Stephen A. Conrad, "Putting Rights Talk in Its Place: The *Summary View* Revisited," in Peter S. Onuf, ed., *Jeffersonian Legacies* (Charlottesville, 1993), 254–280.

62. I here follow Maier's division of the grievances into three groups (Maier, *American Scripture,* 107–123), rather than Wills's division into four (Wills, *Inventing America,* 65–75).

63. Sidney Kaplan, "The 'Domestic Insurrections' of the Declaration of Independence," *Journal of Negro History,* 61 (1976), 243–255.

64. Eliga H. Gould, *The Persistence of Empire: British Political Culture in the Age of the American Revolution* (Chapel Hill, 2000), 190–192; Gould, "Zones of Law, Zones of Violence: The Legal Geography of the British Atlantic, circa 1772," *William and Mary Quarterly,* 3rd ser., 60 (2003), 471–510.

65. Jefferson, "Notes of Proceedings in the Continental Congress," in *The Papers of Thomas Jefferson,* ed. Boyd, I, 315.

66. Compare Edwin Gittleman, "Jefferson's 'Slave Narrative': The Declaration of Independence as a Literary Text," *Early American Literature,* 8 (1974), 239–256.

67. [Jefferson,] *A Summary View of the Rights of British America,* 17 (adopting Jefferson's manuscript emendation of "African" to "British" corsairs: *The Papers of Thomas Jefferson,* ed. Boyd, I, 130, 136n24).

68. Treaty of Amity and Commerce (February 6, 1778), Article VIII, in *The Treaties of 1778 and Allied Documents,* ed. Gilbert Chinard (Baltimore, 1928), 28. On early American relations with the Barbary states see Ray W. Irwin, *The Diplomatic Relations of the United States with the Barbary Powers, 1776–1816* (Chapel Hill, 1931); Robert J. Allison, *The Crescent Obscured: The United States and the Muslim World, 1776–1815* (New York, 1995); Frank Lambert, *The Barbary Wars: American Independence in the Atlantic World* (New York, 2005).

69. Compare Peter S. Onuf, *Jefferson's Empire: The Language of American Nationhood* (Charlottesville, 2000), 148–151, 155–158.

70. Thomas Jefferson, *Notes on the State of Virginia* (1785), ed. William Peden (Chapel Hill, 1954), 138.

71. Anne Pérotin-Dumon, "The Pirate and the Emperor: Power and Law on the Seas, 1450–1850," in James Tracy, ed., *The Political Economy of Merchant Empires: State Power and World Trade, 1350–1750* (Cambridge, 1991), 202–203, 215.

72. See Istvan Hont, *Jealousy of Trade: International Competition and the Nation-State in Historical Perspective* (Cambridge, MA, 2005).

73. *Observations on the American Revolution, Published According to a Resolution of Congress, by Their Committee* (Philadelphia, 1779), 122.

74. Ezra Stiles, *The United States Elevated to Glory and Honour,* 2nd ed. (Worcester, MA, 1785), 88–89 and note; Holden Furber, "The Beginnings of American Trade with India, 1784–1812," *New England Quarterly,* 11 (1938), 235–265.

2. The Declaration of Independence in the World

1. Woodrow Wilson, "A Fourth of July Address" (July 4, 1914), in *The Papers of Woodrow Wilson,* gen. ed. Arthur S. Link, 69 vols. (Princeton, 1966–1994), XXX, 250.

2. James Wilson to Robert Morris, January 14, 1777, quoted in James H. Hutson, *John Adams and the Diplomacy of the American Revolution* (Lexington, KY, 1981), 153.

3. John C. Rainbolt, "Americans' Initial View of Their Revolution's Significance for Other Peoples, 1776–1778," *The Historian,* 35 (1973), 426–433.

4. J. G. A. Pocock, "Political Thought in the English-Speaking Atlantic: I, The Imperial Crisis," in Pocock, ed., *The Varieties of British Political Thought, 1500–1800* (Cambridge, 1995), 281; compare Pocock, "States, Republics, and Empires: The American Founding in Early Modern Perspective," in Terence Ball and J. G. A. Pocock, eds., *Conceptual Change and the Constitution* (Lawrence, KS, 1988), 55–77; Edward Dumbauld, "Independence under International Law," *American Journal of International Law,* 70 (1976), 425–431; Peter S. Onuf, "A Declaration of Independence for Diplomatic Historians," *Diplomatic History,* 22 (1998), 71–72, 82–83.

5. [John Adams,] *A Collection of State-Papers, Relative to the Acknowledgement of the Sovereignity [sic] of the United States of America* (The Hague, 1782), 4; "A Fourth of July Tribute to Jefferson" (July 4, 1789), in *The Papers of Thomas Jefferson,* gen. ed. Julian P. Boyd, 31 vols. to date (Princeton, 1950–), XV, 240; David Ramsay, *The History of the American Revolution,* 2 vols. (Philadelphia, 1789), I, 340; John Quincy Adams, *An Address, Delivered at the Request of the Committee of Arrangements for Celebrating the Anniversary of Independence, at the City of Washington on the Fourth of July 1821* (Cambridge, MA, 1821), 11; John C. Calhoun, *A Discourse on the Constitution and Government of the United States,* in *Union and Liberty: The Political Philosophy of John C. Calhoun,* ed. Ross M. Lence (Indianapolis, 1992), 90.

6. R. R. Palmer, *The Age of the Democratic Revolution,* 2 vols. (Princeton, 1959–1964); David Armstrong, *Revolution and World Order: The Revolutionary State in International Society* (Oxford, 1993), chaps. 2–3; Mlada Bukovansky, *Legitimacy and Power Politics: The American and French Revolutions in International Political Culture* (Princeton, 2002).

7. [Friedrich Gentz,] *The Origin and Principles of the American Revolution, Compared with the Origin and Principles of the French Revolution,* trans. John Quincy Adams (Philadelphia, 1800), 41, 55, 59.

8. Peter Onuf and Nicholas Onuf, *Federal Union, Modern World: The Law of Nations in an Age of Revolutions, 1776–1814* (Madison, 1993), 2.

9. G. F. von Martens, *Summary of the Law of Nations, Founded on the Treaties and Customs of the Modern Nations of Europe* (1789), Eng. trans. William Cobbett (Philadelphia, 1795), 2–3.

10. Thomas Jefferson, "Opinions on the French Treaties" (April 28, 1793), in *Papers of Thomas Jefferson,* gen. ed. Boyd, XXV, 609.

11. *Gazeta Warszawska* (Warsaw), September 11, 1776; Irene M. Sokol, "The American Revolution and Poland: A Bibliographical Essay," *Polish Review,* 12 (1967), 8.

12. *Morning Chronicle* (London), August 14, 1776; *British Chronicle* (London), August 14–16, 1776; *St James's Chronicle* (London), *General Evening Post* (London), August 15, 1776; *The Annual Register . . . for the*

Year 1776 (London, 1777), 261–264; D. D., "London Newspapers of 1776 and the Declaration of Independence," *The Nation,* 66 (February 17, 1898), 127–128; Solomon Lutnick, *The American Revolution and the British Press, 1775–1783* (Columbia, MO, 1967), 75–76.

13. *Caledonian Mercury* (Edinburgh), August 20, 1776; Donald W. Livingston, "Hume, English Barbarism and American Independence," in Richard B. Sher and Jeffrey R. Smitten, eds., *Scotland and America in the Age of Enlightenment* (Princeton, 1990), 133; *Freeman's Journal* (Dublin), August 24, 1776.

14. *Gaceta de Madrid* (Madrid), August 27, 1776; Luis Angel García Melero, *La Independencia de los Estados Unidos de Norteamérica a través de la prensa española: los precedentes (1763–1776)* (Madrid, 1977), 296–297; *Gazette de Leyde* (Leiden), August 30, 1776; Jeremy D. Popkin, *News and Politics in the Age of Revolution: Jean Luzac's "Gazette de Leyde"* (Ithaca, NY, 1989), 151; *Wienerisches Diarium* (Vienna), August 31, 1776; Paula S. Fichtner, "Viennese Perspectives on the War of Independence," in Béla K. Király and George Barany, eds., *East Central European Perceptions of Early America* (Lisse, 1977), 20.

15. *Berlingske Tidende* (Copenhagen), September 2, 1776, reproduced in *Independence Documents of the World,* ed. Albert P. Blaustein, Jay Sigler, and Benjamin R. Breede, 2 vols. (New York, 1977), I, 187; *Gazzetta Universale o Sieno Notizie Istoriche, Politiche, di Scienze, Arti, Agricoltura* (Florence) and *Notizie del Mondo* (Florence), September 14, 1776; *Ephemeriden der Menschheit* (Basel), October 1776, 96–106.

16. Harold Nicolson, *Diplomacy,* 2nd ed. (London, 1950), 124–136.

17. Jonathan R. Dull, *A Diplomatic History of the American Revolution* (New Haven, 1985), 15–22; Bingdi He, *Studies on the Population of China, 1368–1953* (Cambridge, MA, 1959), 281.

18. John Adams to the President of Congress, September 5, 1780, in *The Works of John Adams,* ed. Charles Francis Adams, 10 vols. (Boston, 1852), VII, 250.

19. *The Whitefoord Papers: Being the Correspondence and Other Manuscripts of*

Colonel Charles Whitefoord and Caleb Whitefoord, from 1739 to 1810, ed. W. A. S. Hewins (Oxford, 1898), 187.

20. *Pennsylvanischer Staatsbote* (Philadelphia), July 9, 1776; Karl J. R. Arndt, "The First German Broadside and Newspaper Printing of the Declaration of Independence," *Pennsylvania Folklife,* 35 (1986), 98–107; Gerd-J. Bötte, "Der Erstdruck der amerikanischen Unabhängigkeiterklärung in Deutscher sprache (Philadelphia: Steiner und Cist, 1776)," in *Unabhängigkeiterklärung der Vereinigten Staaten von Amerika, 4. Juli 1776, Mitteilungen des Deutschen Historischen Museums,* 3, 9 (Berlin, 1994), 22–26.

21. Richard B. Morris, "The Declaration Was Proclaimed but Few in Europe Listened at First," *Smithsonian,* 6, 4 (July 1975), 30–36.

22. Guy Johnson to Lord George Germain, August 9, 1776, The National Archives (hereafter, TNA), Kew, CO 5/177/113. See generally Howard H. Peckham, "Independence: The View from Britain," *Proceedings of the American Antiquarian Society,* 85 (1976), 387–403.

23. Vincent Morley, *Irish Opinion and the American Revolution, 1760–1783* (Cambridge, 2002), 148–150.

24. Edmund Burke, "Speech on Army Estimates" (December 14, 1778), in *The Writings and Speeches of Edmund Burke,* III: *Party, Parliament, and the American War, 1774–1780,* ed. Warren M. Elofson and John A. Woods (Oxford, 1996), 394.

25. *The American Journal of Ambrose Serle, Secretary to Lord Howe, 1776–1778,* ed. Edward H. Tatum, Jr. (San Marino, CA, 1940), 31.

26. "Lord Howe's Conference with the Committee of Congress" (September 11, 1776), in *The Papers of Benjamin Franklin,* gen. ed. Leonard W. Labaree et al., 37 vols. to date (New Haven, 1959–), XXII, 600.

27. TNA ADM 1/487/34 (Philadelphia: John Dunlap); CO 5/40/252 (Philadelphia: John Dunlap); CO 5/177/29 (Philadelphia: John Dunlap); CO 5/1107/375 (New York: Hugh Gaine); CO 5/1353/401 (Baltimore: John Dunlap). Only one of these five copies is recorded in M. J. Walsh, "Contemporary Broadside Editions of the

Declaration of Independence," *Harvard Library Bulletin,* 3 (1949), 31–43, and only two in Frederick R. Goff, *The John Dunlap Broadside: The First Printing of the Declaration of Independence* (Washington, D.C., 1976), 5, 48–51. No other copy of the Baltimore imprint is recorded.

28. Thomas Hutchinson to Earl of Hardwicke, August 10, 1776, British Library (hereafter, BL), Add. MS 35427, fol. 94r.

29. Bernard Bailyn, *The Ordeal of Thomas Hutchinson* (Cambridge, MA, 1974), 1, 356–359; [Thomas Hutchinson,] *Strictures upon the Declaration of the Congress at Philadelphia, in a Letter to a Noble Lord* (London, 1776). The "Noble Lord" was the Earl of Hardwicke.

30. King George III, "Speech to Both Houses of Parliament" (October 31, 1776), in *The Annual Register . . . for the Year 1777* (London, 1778), 275.

31. *American Archives: Fifth Series . . . From the Declaration of Independence, July 4, 1776, to the Definitive Treaty of Peace with Great Britain, September 3, 1783,* ed. Peter Force, 3 vols. (Washington, D.C., 1848–1853), II, 189.

32. [John Lind and Jeremy Bentham,] *An Answer to the Declaration of the American Congress* (London, 1776), 5.

33. [John Lind and Jeremy Bentham,] *Remarks on the Principal Acts of the Thirteenth Parliament* (London, 1775); [Lind,] *Three Letters to Dr Price, Containing Remarks on his Observations on the Nature of Civil Liberty, the Principles of Government, and the Justice and Policy of the War with America* (London, 1776); Margaret E. Avery, "Toryism in the Age of the American Revolution: John Lind and John Shebbeare," *Historical Studies* (Melbourne), 18 (1978), 24–36.

34. Peckham, "Independence: The View from Britain," 399. The sole surviving copy of the original version of the *Answer to the Declaration* is in the John Carter Brown Library, Providence, RI, call number A41c. It has Bentham's inscription on the title page: "This is the work in its original state. A considerable part of this was left out at the desire of the Ministry in the published copy."

35. William Knox to Sir William Howe, November 6, 1776, TNA CO 5/93, fol. 290.

36. [Lind and Bentham,] *Answer to the Declaration of the American Congress,* 6–7, 95, 107.

37. [Hutchinson,] *Strictures upon the Declaration of the Congress at Philadelphia,* 9–10; Thomas Day, *Fragment of an Original Letter on the Slavery of the Negroes; Written in the Year 1776* (London, 1784), 33. See also *An Appeal to Reason and Justice in Behalf of the British Constitution and the Subjects of the British Empire* (London, 1778), 76–78.

38. [Louis-Alexandre de La Rochefoucauld d'Enville,] "Lettre d'un banquier de Londres à M.——, à Anvers" (September 2, 1776), *Affaires de l'Angleterre et de l'Amérique,* 15 vols. (Antwerp, 1776–1779), tome I, cahier VIII, 89–92; ibid., tome I, cahier VII, 88; translated as "The Declaration in France," in Robert Ginsberg, ed., *A Casebook on the Declaration of Independence* (New York, 1967), 18–20.

39. [Hutchinson,] *Strictures upon the Declaration of the Congress at Philadelphia,* 9–10; "An Englishman," *The Scots Magazine,* 38 (August 1776), 433–434.

40. [Joseph Peart,] *A Continuation of Hudibras in Two Cantos. Written in the Time of the Unhappy Contest between Great Britain and America, in 1777 and 1778* (London, 1778), 62–63.

41. [Jeremy Bentham,] "Short Review of the Declaration," in [Lind and Bentham,] *Answer to the Declaration of the American Congress,* 120.

42. Jeremy Bentham to John Lind, September 1776, "American Declaration. Hints B.," BL Add. MS 33551, fols. 359r–60v, printed in *The Correspondence of Jeremy Bentham,* gen. ed. Timothy L. S. Sprigge, 12 vols. to date (London and Oxford, 1968–), vol. I, 341–344; Douglas J. Long, *Bentham on Liberty: Jeremy Bentham's Idea of Liberty in Relation to His Utilitarianism* (Toronto, 1977), 51–54; H. L. A. Hart, "The United States of America," in Hart, *Essays on Bentham: Jurisprudence and Political Theory* (Oxford, 1982), 63–65.

43. Jeremy Bentham, "Hey" (1776), Bentham Papers, University College London, LXIX, 57–68, replying to [Richard Hey,] *Observations, on the*

Nature of Civil Liberty, and the Principles of Government (London, 1776); Long, *Bentham on Liberty,* 57–61; G. I. Molivas, "A Right, Utility and the Definition of Liberty as a Negative Idea: Richard Hey and the Benthamite Conception of Liberty," *History of European Ideas,* 25 (1999), 75–92.

44. Jeremy Bentham, *An Introduction to the Principles of Morals and Legislation* (1780/89), ed. J. H. Burns and H. L. A. Hart, Intro. F. Rosen (Oxford, 1996), 311, note; *The Works of Jeremy Bentham,* ed. John Bowring, 11 vols. (Edinburgh, 1838– 1843), X, 63.

45. Jeremy Bentham, "Nonsense upon Stilts" (1792), in Bentham, *Rights, Representation, and Reform: Nonsense upon Stilts and Other Writings on the French Revolution,* ed. Philip Schofield, Catherine Pease-Watkin, and Cyprian Blamires (Oxford, 2002), 330.

46. Jacques Derrida, "Déclarations d'Indépendance" (1976), in Derrida, *Otobiographies: L'enseignement de Nietzsche et la politique du nom propre* (Paris, 1984), 31; Derrida, "Declarations of Independence," *New Political Science,* 15 (1986), 13.

47. Jeremy Bentham, *A Fragment on Government* (1776), ed. J. H. Burns and H. L. A. Hart, Intro. Ross Harrison (Cambridge, 1988), 47.

48. Instructions to Benjamin Franklin, Silas Deane, and Arthur Lee (September 24–October 22, 1776), Houghton Library, Harvard University, bMS 811. 1 (81–83).

49. Committee of Secret Correspondence to Silas Deane, July 8, 1776, in *Letters of Delegates to Congress, 1774–1789,* gen. ed. Paul H. Smith, 26 vols. to date (Washington, D.C., 1976–), IV, 405; Pauline Maier, *American Scripture: Making the Declaration of Independence* (New York, 1997), 130.

50. *Journal historique et politique* (Paris), September 10, 1776; *Affaires de l'Angleterre et de l'Amérique,* tome I, cahier 7, 88–95; ibid., tome 9, 169–177; [Régnier,] *Recueil des loix constitutives des colonies angloises, confédérées sous la dénomination de l'Amérique-Septentrionale* (Paris, 1778), 3–13; [Louis-Alexandre de La Rochefoucauld d'Enville,] *Con-*

stitutions des treize Etats-Unis de l'Amérique (Paris, 1783), 419–429; Durand Echeverria, "French Publications of the Declaration of Independence and the American Constitutions, 1776–1783," *Papers of the Bibliographical Society of America*, 47 (1953), 317–323.

51. R. R. Palmer, "The Declaration of Independence in France," *Studies on Voltaire and the Eighteenth Century*, 154 (1976), 1569–1579; Naomi Wulf and Elise Marienstras, "Traduire, emprunter, adapter la déclaration d'indépendance des Etats-Unis. Transferts et malentendus dans les traductions françaises," *Dix-Huitième Siècle*, 33 (2001), 201–218.

52. Treaty of Alliance (February 6, 1778), Article II, in *The Treaties of 1778 and Allied Documents*, ed. Gilbert Chinard (Baltimore, 1928), 52: "la liberté, la souveraineté, et l'indépendance absolue et illimité des dis Etats unis."

53. [Edward Gibbon,] "Mémoire justificatif pour servir de réponse a l'exposé des motifs de la conduite du roi de France relativement a l'Angleterre," in *The Miscellaneous Works of Edward Gibbon, Esq.*, ed. John, Lord Sheffield, 5 vols. (London, 1814), V, 3, 27–28, 33 (my translations).

54. [John Wilkes,] *A Supplement to the Miscellaneous Works of Edward Gibbon, Esq.* (n.p., n.d. [London, 1796]), 4, 13.

55. On the contemporary context of these issues see Julius Goebel, Jr., *The Recognition Policy of the United States* (New York, 1915), chap. III, "Intervention and Recognition in the American Revolution."

56. C. H. Alexandrowicz, "The Theory of Recognition *in Fieri*," *British Year Book of International Law*, 34 (1958), 176–198; James Crawford, *The Creation of States in International Law* (Oxford, 1979), 5–12; Wilhelm Grewe, *The Epochs of International Law*, rev. and trans. Michael Byers (Berlin, 2000), 343–348.

57. J. C. W. von Steck, "Versuch von Erkennung der Unabhängigkeit einer Nation, und eines Staats," in Steck, *Versuche über verschiedene*

Materien politischer und rechtlicher Kenntnisse (Berlin, 1783), 49–56; Alexandrowicz, "Theory of Recognition *in Fieri*," 180–184.

58. Martens, *Summary of the Law of Nations*, trans. Cobbett, 80 and note; Alexandrowicz, "Theory of Recognition *in Fieri*," 184–187.

59. Charles de Martens, *Nouvelles causes célèbres du droit des gens*, 2 vols. (Leipzig, 1843), I, 113–209, 370–498.

60. "Article I," *The Definitive Treaty of Peace and Friendship Between His Britannick Majesty, and the United States of America* (September 3, 1783) (London, 1783), 4.

61. *The Works and Correspondence of the Right Honourable Edmund Burke*, ed. Charles William, Earl Fitzwilliam, and Sir Richard Bourke, 2nd ed., 7 vols. (London, 1852), II, 453.

62. "Cette indépendance est reconnue, assurée; [nos politiques] semblent la voir avec indifférence": Marie-Jean Antoine-Nicolas Caritat, Marquis de Condorcet, "De l'Influence de la Révolution d'Amérique sur l'Europe" (1786), in *Oeuvres de Condorcet*, ed. A. Condorcet O'Connor and M. F. Arago, 12 vols. (Paris, 1847–1849), VIII, 3.

63. Charles Jenkinson, *A Collection of All the Treaties of Peace, Alliance, and Commerce between Great-Britain and Other Powers, From the Treaty Signed at Munster in 1649, to the Treaties Signed at Paris in 1783*, 3 vols. (London, 1785), I, iii; III, 237–241.

64. "List of the Principal Treaties . . . Between the Different Powers of Europe since the Year 1748 down to the Present Time," in Martens, *Summary of the Law of Nations*, trans. Cobbett, 362; Martens, *Recueil des principaux traités d'alliance, de paix, de trève, de neutralité, de commerce*, 5 vols. (Göttingen, 1791–1807), I, 580; Martens, *Recueil de traités de paix . . . et de plusieurs autres actes servant à la connaissance des relations étrangères des puissances et états de l'Europe*, 8 vols. (Göttingen, 1817–1835), II, 481–485 (Declaration); 486–502 (Articles of Confederation).

65. James Kent, *Commentaries on American Law*, 4 vols. (New York, 1828), I, 2; M. W. Janis, "American Versions of the International Law of Christendom: Kent, Wheaton and the Grotian Tradition," *Netherlands*

International Law Review, 39 (1992), 38–39. On the relationship of American municipal law to international law in this period see Stewart Jay, "The Status of the Law of Nations in Early American Law," *Vanderbilt Law Review,* 42 (1989), 819–849.

66. On the history of this tradition see especially Knud Haakonssen, *Natural Law and Moral Philosophy: From Grotius to the Scottish Enlightenment* (Cambridge, 1996); Haakonssen, ed., *Grotius, Pufendorf and Modern Natural Law* (Aldershot, 1999); T. J. Hochstrasser, *Natural Law Theories in the Early Enlightenment* (Cambridge, 2000).

67. Jeremy Waldron, *"Nonsense Upon Stilts": Bentham, Burke and Marx on the Rights of Man* (London, 1987), 18; compare Lynn Hunt, "The Paradoxical Origins of Human Rights," in Jeffrey N. Wasserstrom, Lynn Hunt, and Marilyn B. Young, eds., *Human Rights and Revolutions* (Lanham, 2000), 3–17.

68. *The Federal and State Constitutions, Colonial Charters and Other Organic Laws of the States, Territories, and Colonies Now or Heretofore Forming the United States of America,* ed. Francis Newton Thorpe, 7 vols. (Washington, D.C., 1909), III, 1686 (Maryland); V, 2789 (North Carolina); V, 3081 (Pennsylvania); II, 778 (Georgia); VI, 3248 (South Carolina); V, 2625–2628 (New York); III, 1889 (Massachusetts); VII, 3813 (Virginia); Maier, *American Scripture,* 165–167.

69. *Records of the Council of Safety and Governor and Council of the State of Vermont,* ed. E. P. Walton, 8 vols. (Montpelier, VT, 1873–1880), I, 40–44 (January 15, 1777).

70. Stephen R. Bradley, *Vermont's Appeal to the Candid and Impartial World* (Hartford, CT, 1780), 30.

71. Quoted in Peter S. Onuf, "State-Making in Revolutionary America: Independent Vermont as a Case Study," *Journal of American History,* 67 (1981), 801.

72. Steven R. Ratner, "Drawing a Better Line: *Uti Possidetis* and the Borders of New States," *American Journal of International Law,* 90 (1996), 590. The term derives from the Latin phrase "uti possidetis, ita possideatis": "as you possess, so may you possess."

73. Philip F. Detweiler, "The Changing Reputation of the Declaration of Independence: The First Fifty Years," *William and Mary Quarterly,* 3rd ser., 19 (1962), 557–574; Maier, *American Scripture,* 170–189; Alfred F. Young, *The Shoemaker and the Tea Party* (Boston, 1999), 111–112, 140, 146–148; Andrew Burstein, *America's Jubilee* (New York, 2001); Irma B. Jaffe, *John Trumbull: Patriot-Artist of the American Revolution* (Boston, 1975); William R. Coleman, "Counting the Stones: A Census of the Stone Facsimiles of the Declaration of Independence," *Manuscripts,* 43 (1991), 97–105; Thomas Starr, "Separated at Birth: Text and Context of the Declaration of Independence," *Proceedings of the American Antiquarian Society,* 110 (2000), 188–194.

74. Len Travers, *Celebrating the Fourth: Independence Day and the Rites of Nationalism in the Early Republic* (Amherst, MA, 1997), 21–23, 161, 206; David Waldstreicher, *In the Midst of Perpetual Fetes: The Making of American Nationalism, 1776–1820* (Chapel Hill, 1997), 30–35, 99–102, 206–207, 219–229, 240, 311–313; Maier, *American Scripture,* 160, 191 (quoted).

75. Sándor Bölöni Farkas, *Útazás Észak Amerikában* (Kolozsvár, 1834), 90–98; Farkas, *Journey in North America,* trans. Theodore and Helen Benedek Schoenman (Philadelphia, 1977), 86; Alfred A. Reisch, "Sándor Bölöni Farkas's Reflections on American Political and Social Institutions," in Béla K. Király and George Barany, eds., *East Central European Perceptions of Early America* (Lisse, 1977), 59–72.

76. Adams, *An Address, Delivered . . . on the Fourth of July 1821,* 28.

77. *We, the Other People: Alternative Declarations of Independence by Labor Groups, Farmers, Woman's Rights Advocates, Socialists, and Blacks, 1829–1975,* ed. Philip S. Foner (Urbana, 1976), 2–5, 47–50.

78. "Declaration of Independence," *South African Christian Recorder,* 2, 8 (January 1837), 432, reprinted from *Sabbath School Visiter* (Boston), 4 (August 1836).

79. *Declaration of Principles, Comprised in the Address and Resolutions of the Native American Convention, Assembled at Philadelphia, July 4, 1845* (Philadelphia, 1845), partially reprinted in *The Ordeal of Assimilation: A Doc-*

umentary History of the White Working Class, ed. Stanley Feldstein and Lawrence Costello (Garden City, 1974), 146–153.

80. [Elizabeth Cady Stanton,] "Declaration of Sentiments" (July 19, 1845), in *We, the Other People,* ed. Foner, 78–81.

81. Philip F. Detweiler, "Congressional Debate on Slavery and the Declaration of Independence, 1819–1821," *American Historical Review,* 63 (1958), 598–616.

82. George Fitzhugh, *Cannibals All! Or, Slaves without Masters* (1857), ed. C. Vann Woodward (Cambridge, MA, 1960), 133.

83. George Fitzhugh, "Revolutions of '76 and '61 Contrasted" (1863), *De Bow's Review,* After the War ser., 4 (1867), 37.

84. Abraham Lincoln, "Speech at Springfield, Illinois" (June 26, 1857), Lincoln to Henry L. Pierce and Others, April 6, 1859, in *The Collected Works of Abraham Lincoln,* ed. Roy P. Basler, 9 vols. (New Brunswick, NJ, 1953–1955), II, 407; III, 376; Merrill D. Peterson, *"This Grand Pertinacity": Abraham Lincoln and the Declaration of Independence* (Fort Wayne, 1991); Garry Wills, *Lincoln at Gettysburg: The Words That Remade America* (New York, 1992), 99–132.

85. Herbert Aptheker, *"One Continual Cry": David Walker's "Appeal to the Colored Citizens of the World" (1829–1830): Its Setting, Its Meaning* (New York, 1965), 142–143.

86. Frederick Douglass, "What to the Slave is the Fourth of July?: An Address Delivered in Rochester, New York, on 5 July 1852," in *The Frederick Douglass Papers,* ed. John W. Blassingame, 5 vols. (New Haven, 1979–1992), II, 360, 363, 368, 371; James A. Colaiaco, *Frederick Douglass and the Fourth of July* (New York, 2006).

87. Douglass, "What to the Slave is the Fourth of July?" in *The Frederick Douglass Papers,* ed. Blassingame, II, 382–383.

88. Douglass, "What to the Slave is the Fourth of July?," in *The Frederick Douglass Papers,* ed. Blassingame, II, 387.

89. On nineteenth-century globalization see especially Kevin H. O'Rourke and Jeffrey G. Williamson, *Globalization and History: The Evolution of a Nineteenth-Century Atlantic Economy* (Cambridge, MA,

1999); Duncan S. A. Bell, "Dissolving Distance: Technology, Space, and Empire in British Political Thought, 1770–1900," *Journal of Modern History,* 77 (2005), 523–562.

90. C. A. Bayly, *The Making of the Modern World, 1780–1914* (Oxford, 2004), chaps. 3, 6, 7.

91. Homer L. Calkin, "The Centenary of American Independence 'Round the World," *The Historian,* 38 (1975–1976), 614–616.

3. A World of Declarations

1. C. H. Alexandrowicz, "New and Original States: The Issue of Reversion to Sovereignty," *International Affairs,* 45 (1969), 465–480.

2. On these moments see Jordana Dym, "'Our Pueblos, Fractions with No Central Unity': Municipal Sovereignty in Central America, 1808–1821," *Hispanic American Historical Review,* 86 (2006), 431–466; Joshua B. Hill, "A Question of Independence: Rhetoric and Crisis in a Chinese City, 1911–1917" (AM thesis, Harvard University, 2005); Frank Hoffman, "The Muo Declaration: History in the Making (Translation and Commentary)," *Korean Studies,* 13 (1989), 22–41.

3. Giorgio Agamben, *State of Exception,* trans. Kevin Attell (Chicago, 2005).

4. Frederick Cooper, "States, Empires, and Political Imagination," in Cooper, *Colonialism in Question: Theory, Knowledge, History* (Berkeley, 2005), 190; David Strang, "Global Patterns of Decolonization, 1500–1987," *International Studies Quarterly,* 35 (1991), 429–454.

5. Victor Lieberman, *Strange Parallels: Southeast Asia in Global Context, c. 800–1830,* I: *Integration on the Mainland* (Cambridge, 2003), 2.

6. Mark Greengrass, "Introduction: Conquest and Coalescence," in Greengrass, ed., *Conquest and Coalescence: The Shaping of the State in Early Modern Europe* (London, 1991), 1–2.

7. Mary Ann Glendon, *A World Made New: Eleanor Roosevelt and the Universal Declaration of Human Rights* (New York, 2001), 245n24.

8. <http://www.un.org/Overview/growth.htm>, accessed July 4, 2006.

9. Ernest Gellner, *Nations and Nationalism* (London, 1983), 2, 44–45, 139–140.

10. Charles Maier, "Empires or Nations? 1918, 1945, 1989 . . . ," in Carl Levy and Mark Roseman, eds., *Three Postwar Eras in Comparison: Western Europe, 1918–1945–1989* (Basingstoke, 2002), 50; Maier, *Among Empires: American Ascendancy and Its Predecessors* (Cambridge, MA, 2006), chaps. 1–2.

11. Edward Keene, *Beyond the Anarchical Society: Grotius, Colonialism and Order in World Politics* (Cambridge, 2002), 5–6, 97, 143–144.

12. Nicholas Greenwood Onuf, "Sovereignty: Outline of a Conceptual History," *Alternatives,* 16 (1991), 430; compare Thomas J. Biersteker and Cynthia Weber, eds., *State Sovereignty as Social Construct* (Cambridge, 1996).

13. ". . . les droits des hommes furent hautement soutenus et développés sans restriction, sans réserve, dans des écrits qui circulaient avec liberté des bords de la Néva à ceux du Guadalquivir": Marie-Jean Antoine-Nicolas Caritat, Marquis de Condorcet, "Esquisse d'un Tableau historique des progrès de l'esprit humain" (1795), in *Oeuvres de Condorcet,* ed. A. Condorcet O'Connor and M. F. Arago, 12 vols. (Paris, 1847–1849), VI, 199.

14. P. M. Kitromilides, "An Enlightenment Perspective on Balkan Cultural Pluralism: The Republican Vision of Rhigas Velestinlis," *History of Political Thought,* 24 (2003), 465–479; *The Movement for Greek Independence, 1770–1821: A Collection of Documents,* ed. Richard Clogg (London, 1976), 149–163.

15. "Declaration of Independence" (January 15, 1822), in John L. Comstock, *History of the Greek Revolution* (New York, 1828), 499–500.

16. C. A. Bayly, *The Making of the Modern World, 1780–1814* (Oxford, 2004), 86–87, 293–294; Bayly, "Rammohan Roy and the Advent of Constitution Liberalism in India, 1800–30," *Modern Intellectual History,* 4 (2007).

17. ". . . L'acte qui a déclaré son indépendance est une exposition simple et sublime de ces droits si sacrés et si longtemps oubliés": Marie-Jean

Antoine-Nicolas Caritat, Marquis de Condorcet, "De l'Influence de la Révolution d'Amérique sur l'Europe" (1786), in *Oeuvres de Condorcet,* ed. Condorcet O'Connor and Arago, VIII, 11.

18. On the global extent of this moment see Rudolf von Albertini, "The Impact of Two World Wars on the Decline of Colonialism," *Journal of Contemporary History,* 4 (1969), 17–26; John Gallagher, "Nationalisms and the Crisis of Empire, 1919–1922," *Modern Asian Studies,* 15 (1981), 355–368; Erez Manela, *The Wilsonian Moment: Self-Determination and the International Origins of Anticolonial Nationalism* (New York, forthcoming).

19. Quoted in Karen Knop, *Diversity and Self-Determination in International Law* (Cambridge, 2002), 282.

20. David Hunter Miller, *The Drafting of the Covenant,* 2 vols. (New York, 1928), I, 183–184.

21. George J. Kovtun, *The Czechoslovak Declaration of Independence: A History of the Document* (Washington, D.C., 1985).

22. Antonio Cassese, *Self-Determination of Peoples: A Legal Reappraisal* (Cambridge, 1995), 37.

23. On the origins of this moment see Mark Mazower, "The Strange Triumph of Human Rights, 1933–1950," *The Historical Journal,* 47 (2004), 379–398.

24. "Texto da Proclamação de Independência" (November 11, 1975), in *Angola: Documentos de Independência* (Lisbon, 1976), 7–20; Jill Jolliffe, *East Timor: Nationalism and Colonialism* (St Lucia, Qld., 1978), 199–200, 212 (November 28, 1975).

25. For a useful interim survey of this moment see Roland Rich, "Recognition of States: The Collapse of Yugoslavia and the Soviet Union," *European Journal of International Law,* 4 (1993), 36–63.

26. Marc Weller, *The Crisis in Kosovo, 1989–1999* (Cambridge, 1999), 72; "Trying to Behave Like a Proper State," *The Economist* (U.S. edition), October 1, 2005, 43–44 (on Somaliland).

27. J. F. Rohaert, *Manifeste de la Province de Flandre* (January 4, 1790) (Ghent, 1790), 3.

28. Jean-Nicholas Démeunier, *L'Amérique Indépendante, Ou les différentes Constitutions des treize provinces . . . d'États-Unis de l'Amérique,* 3 vols. (Ghent, 1790), I, 32–37 (translation of Declaration of Independence).

29. ". . . appellant au Juge suprême de l'Univers, qui connoît la droiture de nos intentions, Nous publions et déclarons solemnellement, au nom & et de l'autorité du bon Peuple de ces Colonies; Que ces Colonies sont & ont droit d'être des *Etats libres & indépendans:* Qu'elles sont dégagées de toute obéissance envers la Couronne de la Grande-Bretagne": Démeunier, *L'Amérique Indépendante,* I, 37.

30. ". . . appellant au Juge suprême de l'Univers, qui connoît la Justice de notre Cause, Nous publions & déclarons solemnellement, au nom du Peuple, que cette Province EST & a droit d'ÊTRE un *Etat libre & indépendant;* qu'elle est degagée de toute obéissance envers *l'Empereur Joseph second*": Rohaert, *Manifeste de la Province de Flandre,* 23; Thomas K. Gorman, *America and Belgium: A Study of the Influence of the United States upon the Belgian Revolution of 1789–1790* (London, 1925), 156–157.

31. *Acte d'indépendance des États-Unis de l'Amérique, et constitutions des Républiques française, cisalpine et ligurienne, dans les quatre langues française, allemande, anglaise et italienne* (n.p, n.d. [Paris, 1798]), 2–15; R. R. Palmer, "The Declaration of Independence in France," *Studies on Voltaire and the Eighteenth Century,* 154 (1976), 1574–1579.

32. Thomas Madiou, *Histoire d'Haïti* (1847–1848), 8 vols. (Port-au-Prince, 1989–1991), III, 145; Laurent Dubois, *Avengers of the New World: The Story of the Haitian Revolution* (Cambridge, MA, 2004), 298–299.

33. [Louis Boisrond-Tonnerre,] "Le Général en Chef au Peuple d'Haïti" (January 1, 1804), in Madiou, *Histoire d'Haïti,* III, 146–150; Eng. trans., Marcus Rainsford, *An Historical Account of the Black Empire of Hayti: Comprehending a View of the Principal Transactions in the Revolution of Saint-Domingo; with its Ancient and Modern State* (London, 1805), 442–446.

34. Donald R. Hickey, "America's Response to the Slave Revolt in Haiti,

1791–1806," *Journal of the Early Republic,* 2 (1982), 361–379; Tim Matthewson, "Jefferson and the Nonrecognition of Haiti," *Proceedings of the American Philosophical Society,* 140 (1996), 22–48.

35. Jean-François Brière, "La France et la reconnaissance de l'indépendance haïtienne: le débat sur l'ordonnance de 1825," *French Colonial History,* 5 (2004), 125–138.

36. "Act of the Proclamation of the Independence of the Filipino People" (June 12, 1898), in *The Philippine Insurrection against the United States: A Compilation of Documents,* ed. John R. M. Taylor, 5 vols. (Pasay City, 1971), III, 102–106.

37. Arthur Preston Whitaker, *The United States and the Independence of Latin America, 1800–1830* (Baltimore, 1941); James E. Lewis, Jr., *The American Union and the Problem of Neighborhood: The United States and the Collapse of the Spanish Empire, 1783–1829* (Chapel Hill, 1998).

38. Thomas Jefferson to John Jay, May 4, 1787, in *The Papers of Thomas Jefferson,* gen. ed. Julian P. Boyd, 31 vols. to date (Princeton, 1950–), XI, 339–341; Kenneth Maxwell, *Naked Tropics: Essays on Empire and Other Rogues* (London, 2003), 109–10.

39. *Manifesto da Independencia dos Estados Unidos d'America* (Lisbon, 1821).

40. *Manifeste de la nation portugaise aux souvérains et aux peuples de l'Europe* (December 15, 1820) (Lisbon, 1821); Maxwell, *Naked Tropics,* 155–156; Francisco de Assis Cintra, *D. Pedro I e o Grito de Independencia* (São Paulo, 1921), 211–229; Eng. trans., "The Declaration of Brazilian Independence" (January 9, 1822), in *A Documentary History of Brazil,* ed. E. Bradford Burns (New York, 1956), 198–200.

41. Harry Bernstein, *Origins of Inter-American Interest, 1700–1812* (Philadelphia, 1945), 79–80.

42. Richard J. Cleveland, *A Narrative of Voyages and Commercial Enterprises,* 2 vols. (Cambridge, MA, 1842), I, 183–184, 209–210; Miguel de Pombo, *La constitución de los Estados-Unidos de America* (Bogotá, 1811), 1–9; Manuel García de Sena, trans., *La independencia de la Costa Firme justificada por Thomas Paine treinta años há* (Philadelphia, 1811), 157–162; [Vicente Rocafuerte,] *Ideas necesarias á todo pueblo americano*

independiente, que quiera ser libre (Philadelphia, 1821), 3 ("el verdadero decálogo político"), 103–111. See generally Mario Rodríguez, *La revolución americana de 1776 y el mundo hispánico: ensayos y documentos* (Madrid, 1976); Merle E. Simmons, *La revolución norteamericana en la independencia de Hispanoamérica* (Madrid, 1992); Bernard Bailyn, *To Begin the World Anew: The Genius and Ambiguities of the American Founders* (New York, 2003), 146–147.

43. See generally José Luis Romero, "La independencia de Hispanoamérica y el modelo político norteamericano," *Inter-American Review of Bibliography,* 26 (1976), 429–455; Susan Deans and Edward Countryman, "Independence and Revolution in the Americas: A Project for Comparative Study," *Radical History Review,* 27 (1983), 144–171; José Carlos Chiaramonte, "The Principle of Consent in Latin and Anglo-American Independence," *Journal of Latin American Studies,* 36 (2004), 563–586.

44. Jaime E. Rodríguez O., *The Independence of Spanish America* (Cambridge, 1998), 2.

45. P. L. Blanco Peñalver, *Historia y comentarios del Libro de Actas de la independencia de Venezuela 1811* (Caracas, 1983); Rodríguez, *The Independence of Spanish America,* 114–115.

46. "Acta de Independencia" (July 5, 1811), in *Interesting Official Documents Relating to The United Provinces of Venezuela* (London, 1812), 3–21.

47. "Acta de la independencia de la provincia de Cartagena en la Nueva Granada" (November 11, 1811), in *Constituciones de Colombia,* ed. Manuel Antonio Pombo and José Joaquín Guerra, 4th ed., 4 vols. (Bogotá, 1986), II, 75–82; Eng. trans., *British and Foreign State Papers. 1812–1814* (London, 1841), 1136–1142.

48. "Acta de independencia de las Provincias Unidas del Rio de la Plata" (July 9, 1816), in *Registro nacional* (Argentina), 7 (Buenos Aires, 1816), 366–367; Eng. trans., *The Spanish Tradition in America,* ed. Charles Gibson (New York, 1966), 239–240; Bonifacio del Carril, *La Declaración de la independencia* (Buenos Aires, 1966).

49. "Proclamación de la independencia política de Chile" (January 1, 1818), in *Documentos para la historia de la vida pública del libertador de Colombia, Péru y Bolivia,* ed. José Félix Blanco, 14 vols. (Caracas, 1875–1877), VI, 238–239; Eng. trans., *British and Foreign State Papers. 1818–1819* (London, 1835), 820–821; Luis Valencia Avaria, "La Declaración y Proclamación de la Independencia de Chile," *Boletín de la Academia Chilena de la Historia,* 35 (1968), 5–42.

50. José Carlos Chiaramonte, *Nación y Estado en Iberoamérica: El lenguaje político en tiempos de las independencias* (Buenos Aires, 2004).

51. Manuel Montúfar y Coronado, quoted in Dym, "'Our Pueblos, Fractions with no Central Unity,'" 464.

52. "Proclamacion y juramento de la independencia" (July 15, 1821), in *Documentos para la historia de la vida pública del libertador,* ed. Blanco, VIII, 5–7; Eng. trans., *British and Foreign State Papers. 1821–1822* (London, 1829), 393–394; Timothy E. Anna, "The Peruvian Declaration of Independence: Freedom by Coercion," *Journal of Latin American Studies,* 7 (1975), 221–248.

53. "The Unanimous Declaration of Independence Made by the Delegates of the People of Texas" (March 2, 1836), in *The Papers of the Texas Revolution, 1835–1836,* gen. ed. John H. Jenkins, 10 vols. (Austin, 1973), IV, 493–497.

54. "Acta de Independencia del Imperio" (September 28, 1821), in *El Libertador: Documentos Selectos de D. Agustín de Iturbide,* ed. Mariano Cuevas (Mexico City, 1947), 262–263.

55. "En el Puerto de Monterrey de la Alta California . . ." (November 7, 1836) (Monterey, 1836), reprod. in [Parke-Bernet Galleries,] *The Celebrated Collection of Americana Formed by the Late Thomas Streeter, Morristown, New Jersey,* 8 vols. (New York, 1968), IV, 1781.

56. "Declaration of Independence" (July 26, 1847), in *The Independent Republic of Liberia; Its Constitution and Declaration of Independence . . . with Other Documents; Issued Chiefly for the Use of the Free People of Color* (Philadelphia, 1848), 8–9; Robert W. July, *The Origins of Modern African Thought: Its Development in West Africa during the Nineteenth and Twentieth Centuries* (London, 1967), 93–100.

57. For example, Charles Henry Huberich, *The Political and Legislative History of Liberia*, 2 vols. (New York, 1947), I, 833–834; July, *The Origins of Modern African Thought*, 99.

58. "Declaration of Independence," in *The Independent Republic of Liberia*, 8–9; Gerrit W. Gong, *The Standard of "Civilization" in International Society* (Oxford, 1984).

59. *Kossuth Lajos összes munkái*, 15 vols. (Budapest, 1948–1966), XIV, 894–912; Eng. trans., "Declaration of Independence by the Hungarian Nation" (April 14, 1849), in William H. Stiles, *Austria in 1848–49*, 2 vols. (New York, 1852), II, 409–418; Istvan Deak, *The Lawful Revolution: Louis Kossuth and the Hungarians, 1848–1849* (New York, 1979), 262 (quoted); A. Urbán, "A Lesson for the Old Continent: The Image of America in the Hungarian Revolution of 1848/49," *NHQ; The New Hungarian Quarterly*, 17 (1976), 85–96.

60. György Szabad, "Kossuth on the Political System of the United States of America," *Etudes Hongroises 1975*, 2 vols. (Budapest, 1975), I, 503–529.

61. "Declaration of the Independence of New Zealand" (October 28, 1835), in *Fac-Similes of the Declaration of Independence and the Treaty of Waitangi* (Wellington, NZ, 1877), 4.

62. Busby to the Rev. Mr. Williams and Mr. King, September 14, 1835, and Busby to Colonial Secretary of New South Wales, October 31, 1835, The National Archives, Kew (hereafter TNA), CO 209/2, fols. 88v, 98v; John O. Ross, "Busby and the Declaration of Independence," *New Zealand Journal of History*, 14 (1980), 83–89.

63. Claudia Orange, *The Treaty of Waitangi* (Wellington, NZ, 1987), 118–120.

64. "The Declaration of the Reformers of the City of Toronto to their Fellow Reformers in Upper Canada" (July 31, 1837), in Charles Lindsey, *The Life and Times of Wm. Lyon Mackenzie*, 2 vols. (Toronto, 1863), II, 334–42.

65. [Richard Windeyer,] "On the Rights of the Aborigines of Australia" (June 19, 1844), Mitchell Library, State Library of New South Wales, MS A1400, 2–3; *Sydney Herald,* June 20, 1844

66. John Molony, *Eureka* (Ringwood, 1984), 154; Karl Marx, "The Buying of Commissions.—News from Australia" (March 3, 1855), in Marx and Friedrich Engels, *Collected Works,* 50 vols. (New York, 1975–2004), XIV, 65.

67. Louisa Lawson, "Australian Independence," *The Republican* (Sydney), July 4, 1887.

68. *Official Record of the Proceedings and Debates of the National Australasian Convention . . . March and April 1891* (Sydney, 1891); W. J. Hudson and M. P. Sharp, *Australian Independence: Colony to Reluctant Kingdom* (Melbourne, 1988), 26–27.

69. Marilyn Lake, "What If Alfred Deakin Had Made a Declaration of Australian Independence?" in Stuart Macintyre and Sean Scalmer, eds., *What If? Australian History as It Might Have Been* (Carleton, 2006), 29–43.

70. H. K. Watson, *Whither Australia? Whither Western Australia?* (Perth, Western Australia, 1935); *Report of the Joint Committee of the House of Lords and the House of Commons Appointed to Consider the Petition of the State of Western Australia* (London, 1935); Christopher W. Besant, "Two Nations, Two Destinies: A Reflection on the Significance of the Western Australian Secession Movement to Australia, Canada and the British Empire," *University of Western Australia Law Review,* 20 (1990), 209–310.

71. "Declaration of the Immediate Causes which Induce and Justify the Secession of South Carolina from the Federal Union" (December 20, 1860), in *Journal of the Convention of the People of South Carolina, Held in 1860, 1861 and 1862* (Columbia, SC, 1862), 461–466 (my emphasis).

72. *The War of the Rebellion,* 70 vols. (Washington, D.C., 1880–1901), 4th ser., I, 290 (Tennessee), 741 (Kentucky).

73. See, for example, Francis C. Treadwell, *Secession an Absurdity: It is Perjury, Treason and War* (New York, 1861).

74. Charles and Barbara Jelavich, *The Establishment of the Balkan National*

States, *1804–1920* (Seattle, 1977); T. K. Derry, *A History of Modern Norway, 1814–1972* (Oxford, 1973), 159–171.

75. Cooper, "States, Empires, and Political Imagination," in Cooper, *Colonialism in Question,* 182.

76. Compare Alfred Cobban, *The Nation-State and National Self-Determination,* rev. ed. (London, 1969), 46–49, 101.

77. "Official Declaration of the Republic of Formosa" (May 25, 1895), in James W. Davidson, *The Island of Formosa Past and Present* (London, 1903), 279–280; Harry J. Lamley, "The 1895 Taiwan Republic: A Significant Episode in Modern Chinese History," *Journal of Asian Studies,* 27 (1968), 752, 757.

78. "The Mongolian Proclamation of Independence" (December 11, 1911), in Urgunge Onon and Derrick Pritchatt, *Asia's First Modern Revolution: Mongolia Proclaims Its Independence in 1911* (Leiden, 1989), 126.

79. "The Declaration of Independence of the Czechoslovak Nation" (October 18, 1918), in Kovtun, *The Czechoslovak Declaration of Independence,* 46–48.

80. Thomas G. Masaryk, "The Czecho-Slovak Nation," *The Nation,* 107 (October 5, 1918), 6.

81. "Declaration of Independence of the Mid-European Union" (October 26, 1918), in *International Conciliation,* Special Bulletin (New York, 1919), 23–25; Victor S. Mamatey, *The United States and East Central Europe, 1914–1918: A Study in Wilsonian Diplomacy and Propaganda* (Port Washington, NY, 1957), 342–343.

82. "Proclamation of the State of the Slovenes, Croats and Serbs" (October 29, 1918), in *Yugoslavia through Documents: From Its Creation to Its Dissolution,* ed. Snezana Trifunovska (Dordrecht, 1994), 147–148; *Ireland's Declaration of Independence and Other Official Documents . . . Submitted to the Peace Conference in Support of Ireland's Claim for Recognition as a Sovereign Independent State* (New York, 1919), 3; "The [Korean] Declaration of Independence, March 1, 1919: A

New Translation," *Korean Studies,* 13 (1989), 1–4; "Declaration of Esthonian Independence" (May 19, 1919), TNA, FO 608/186, fols. 229–230.

83. Mahatma Gandhi, "Draft Declaration for January 26 [1930]," and "Things to Remember for the 26th," in *The Collected Works of Mahatma Gandhi,* 90 vols. (New Delhi, 1958–1984), XLII, 384–385, 426–428.

84. Subhas Chandra Bose, "Proclamation of the Provisional Government of Azad Hind" (October 21, 1943), in Hari Hara Das, *Subhas Chandra Bose and the Indian National Movement* (New Delhi, 1983), 367–370.

85. Archimedes L. A. Patti, *Why Viet Nam? Prelude to America's Albatross* (Berkeley, 1980), 223–224.

86. Ho Chi Minh, "Declaration of Independence of the Democratic Republic of Vietnam" (September 2, 1945), in Ho Chi Minh, *Selected Works,* 4 vols. (Hanoi, 1960–1962), III, 17–21; Patti, *Why Viet Nam?,* 250–253; David G. Marr, "Ho Chi Minh's Independence Declaration," in K. W. Taylor and John K. Whitmore, eds., *Essays into Vietnamese Pasts* (Ithaca, 1995), 221–231.

87. Marilyn B. Young, *The Vietnam Wars, 1945–1990* (New York, 1991), 11.

88. [Government of Rhodesia,] "Proclamation" (November 11, 1965), in *Independence Documents of the World,* ed. Albert P. Blaustein, Jay Sigler, and Benjamin R. Beede, 2 vols. (New York, 1977), II, 587.

89. TNA, DO 183/253. The same analogy had been used earlier, in October 1956: TNA, CO 1015/1009.

90. "Declaration on the Granting of Independence to Colonial Countries and Peoples" (December 14, 1960), United Nations, General Assembly Resolution 1514 (XV).

91. Richard M. Cummings, "The Rhodesian Unilateral Declaration of Independence and the Position of the International Community," *New York University Journal of International Law and Politics,* 6 (1973), 57–84; Jericho Nkala, *The United Nations, International Law, and the Rhodesian Independence Crisis* (Oxford, 1985), 43–52.

92. Benedict Anderson, *Imagined Communities: Reflections on the Origin and*

Spread of Nationalism, rev. ed. (London, 1991), 81; compare Adam Watson, "New States in the Americas," in Hedley Bull and Adam Watson, eds., *The Expansion of International Society* (Oxford, 1984), 127–141.

93. Hannah Arendt, *On Revolution* (Harmondsworth, 1973), 56.

Conclusion

1. Gordon S. Wood, *The American Revolution: A History* (New York, 2002), 57.

2. James Crawford, "State Practice and International Law in Relation to Secession," *British Yearbook of International Law,* 69 (1998), 85–117; Perry Anderson, "Stand-Off in Taiwan," *London Review of Books,* June 3, 2004, 15 (quoted).

3. "Proclamation of Independence Order" (April 10, 1971), in *Bangla Desh: Documents* (New Delhi [1971?]), 281–282.

4. "Declaration of the Establishment of the State of Israel" (May 14, 1948), in *Independence Documents of the World,* ed. Albert P. Blaustein, Jay Sigler, and Benjamin R. Beede, 2 vols. (New York, 1977), I, 366–369; Palestine National Council, "Declaration of Independence" (November 15, 1988), in *The Israel-Arab Reader: A Documentary History of the Middle East Conflict,* ed. Walter Laqueur and Barry Rubin, 6th ed. (Harmondsworth, 2001), 354–357; Eliyakim Rubinstein, "The Declaration of Independence as a Basic Document of the State of Israel," *Israel Studies,* 3 (1998), 195–210; James Crawford, "Israel (1948–1949) and Palestine (1998–1999): Two Studies in the Creation of States," in Guy S. Goodwin-Gill and Stefan Talmon, eds., *The Reality of International Law: Essays in Honour of Ian Brownlie* (Oxford, 1999), 95–124.

5. For alternative strategies see Antonio Cassese, *Self-Determination of Peoples: A Legal Reappraisal* (Cambridge, 1995), 344–365; Gerry J. Simpson, "The Diffusion of Sovereignty: Self-Determinations in the Post-Colonial Age," in Mortimer Sellers, ed., *The New World Order: Sovereignty, Human Rights, and the Self-Determination of Peoples* (Oxford,

1996), 35–69; Pekka Aikio and Martin Scheinin, eds., *Operationalizing the Right of Indigenous Peoples to Self-Determination* (Turku, 2000); Marc Weller and Stefan Wolff, eds., *Autonomy, Self-Governance and Conflict Resolution: Innovative Approaches to Institutional Design in Divided Societies* (London, 2005).

Acknowledgments

This is a Harvard book in many senses. I conceived it while I was a Fellow at the university's Charles Warren Center for Studies in American History in response to a well-timed suggestion from Kathleen McDermott of Harvard University Press. The project took longer to complete than Kathleen had hoped or I had expected; her confidence, her patience, and her editing have been indispensable throughout. I presented an early overview of my argument as a lecture to the Harvard History Department and a draft of the manuscript to a Director's Seminar at the Weatherhead Center for International Affairs. On these and many other occasions, colleagues and students in the History Department suggested fertile lines of inquiry and provided crucial leads. I offer the book in modest return for Harvard's outstanding support of those who strive to internationalize and globalize the study of history.

A book that has touched, however briefly, on the histories of so many countries is more than usually dependent on the kindness of friends and, occasionally, strangers. For information, inspiration, and translation, I am variously indebted to Guido Abbattista, Chris Bayly, Manuhuia Barcham, Richard Bourke, Richard Bushman, Thomas Cohen, Laurent Dubois, Karen

Duval, Jordana Dym, Mikulas Fabry, Stella Fitzthomas, Erik Goldner, Joshua Hill, Duncan Ivison, Shruti Kapila, William Kirby, Csaba Lévai, Maria Angela Leal, Charles Maier, Kenneth Maxwell, R. Russell Maylone, Mark Mazower, Wijnand Mijnhardt, Peter Onuf, William O'Reilly, Paul Pickering, John Pocock, Daniel Slive, Glenda Sluga, Miranda Spieler, Simon Stern, Laurel Thatcher Ulrich, Larry Wolff, and John Womack. For opportunities to present versions of my argument to challenging audiences around the world, I am very grateful to Bernard Bailyn, Michael Bess, Michael Braddick, Jeng-Guo Chen, Deborah Cunningham, Jorge Domínguez, Norman Fiering, Andrew Fitzmaurice, James Horn, Akira Iriye, David Johnston, Barbara Ramusack, Tim Rowse, Julia Rudolph, Christopher Saunders, Daniel Sharfstein, Helmut Smith, and Conrad Wright. For their comments on those occasions, I am especially happy to be able to thank Stephen Conway, Frederick Cooper, Christine Desan, Noah Feldman, Eliga Gould, Benedict Kingsbury, James Kloppenberg, Pauline Maier, Susan Marks, Quentin Skinner, and Christopher Tomlins.

Earlier versions of parts of my argument were published in the *William and Mary Quarterly,* the *OAH Magazine of History,* and the *South African Historical Journal.* I am grateful to the editors of all three journals for permission to reproduce material that first appeared in their pages.

I owe special thanks to Bernard Bailyn, Christine Thorsteinsson, Pauline Maier, Darrin McMahon, Erez Manela, and Emma Rothschild for kindly reading the manuscript and for offering invaluable suggestions for improvement.

My greatest debt, as always, is to Joyce Chaplin. She knows why.

Index